What works in assessing community participation?

Danny Burns, Frances Heywood, Pete Wilde and Mandy Wilson

First published in Great Britain in July 2004 by

The Policy Press
Fourth Floor, Beacon House
Queen's Road
Bristol BS8 1QU
UK

Tel no +44 (0)117 331 4054
Fax no +44 (0)117 331 4093
E-mail tpp-info@bristol.ac.uk
www.policypress.org.uk

Published for the Joseph Rowntree Foundation by The Policy Press

ISBN 1 86134 615 8

British Library Cataloguing in Publication Data
A catalogue record for this report is available from the British Library.

Library of Congress Cataloging-in-Publication Data
A catalog record for this report has been requested.

Danny Burns is Professor of Social and Organisational Learning at the University of the West of England, Bristol. **Frances Heywood** is Research Fellow at the School for Policy Studies, University of Bristol. **Pete Wilde** and **Mandy Wilson** are Directors of the COGS Consultancy.

The **Joseph Rowntree Foundation** has supported this project as part of its programme of research and innovative development projects, which it hopes will be of value to policy makers, practitioners and service users. The facts presented and views expressed in this report are, however, those of the authors and not necessarily those of the Foundation.

Cover design by Qube Design Associates, Bristol
Printed in Great Britain by Hobbs the Printers Ltd, Southampton

Contents

Acknowledgements

Special thanks to Peter Marcus of the Joseph Rowntree Foundation who was absolutely essential to supporting and developing this project. Thanks also to John Low of the Joseph Rowntree Foundation for his thoughtful comments and to all of the steering group members, who have included:

Bill Badham, Children's Society, Professor Gary Craig, University of Hull, Naomi Diamond, Engage East Midlands, Scott Dickenson, Audit Commission, Cherida Fletcher, South West Regional Development Agency, Alison Gilchrist, Community Development Foundation, Owen McFarlane, Embrace West Midlands, Ian Matthews, Yorkshire Forward Regional Development Agency, Professor Marjorie Mayo, Goldsmiths College, University of London, Diane Shepherd, Sharrow Community Forum, Caroline Simpson, Advantage West Midlands Regional Development Agency, Hilary Wilmer, Churches Regional Commission, Charles Woodd, Home Office, Active Communities Unit, Tricia Zipfel, Neighbourhood Renewal Unit

The research team

The project was directed by Danny Burns. The research teams were as follows:

The South West

Danny Burns	coordinator
Frances Heywood	action researcher

West Midlands

Paul Burton	coordinator
Carol Ferron-Smith	action researcher

Yorkshire and the Humber

Mandy Wilson	coordinator
Pete Wilde	coordinator
Annie Rosewarne	action researcher
Helen Bovey	action researcher
Kate Jacob	administrator

Advice and support was provided by Marilyn Taylor.

List of abbreviations

BME	black and minority ethnic
COGS	Communities and Organisations: Growth and Support, a community development consultancy run by Pete Wilde and Mandy Wilson
JRF	Joseph Rowntree Foundation
MCTI	Market and Coastal Towns Initiative
MEL	A Birmingham-based consultancy which carried out a section of the road test relating to BME groups
RDA	Regional Development Agency
RMG	Regional Management Group (of the MCTI)
SRB	Single Regeneration Budget
SWRDA	South West Regional Development Agency

Note: Where initials are used, these refer to:

DB	Danny Burns
FH	Frances Heywood
PW	Pete Wilde
MW	Mandy Wilson

Background and context

Background to the road testing

This publication describes and analyses the way in which two tools for benchmarking community involvement in regeneration were road tested. The tools are:

- COGS (2000) *Active partners: Benchmarking community participation in regeneration*, Yorkshire: Yorkshire Forward.
- Burns, D. and Taylor, M. (2000) *Auditing community participation: An assessment handbook*, Bristol: The Policy Press.

The aim of the process was:

(a) to find out if the tools were useful, and to assess what worked most effectively;
(b) to refine the tools and, if possible, amalgamate them on the basis of what we learned from the road-testing process.

As a result of our work, we have produced a combined audit and benchmarking tool, *Making community participation meaningful*, which is published as a companion to this report. The purpose of this publication is to share what was learnt from the road-testing exercise. As we will see, some of the learning relates to the content of the tools themselves, but much of it is about the process of using the tools. It is anticipated that this publication will be read in conjunction with the two original reports (see above), a summary of which can be found later in this chapter (see 'The two assessment frameworks in a nutshell', p 4). These two tools were quite different in their focus, and were used in different ways. Nevertheless, the most important issues about how to use the tools are cross-cutting, and it is for this reason that we have drawn together the learning thematically.

To avoid any danger of confusion about what lessons apply to what tools, we have used the following terminology in the text:

- The Wilde/Wilson (COGS) framework is referred to either as ***Active partners*** or as the **benchmarks**.
- The Burns/Taylor framework is referred to as either the ***Community participation audit*** or as the **audit tools**.
- Where lessons apply to both, we refer to the **assessment frameworks** or **tools**.

One of the early outcomes of the research was that neither 'benchmarking' nor 'audit' are words that are particularly helpful. 'Assessment frameworks' probably comes closer to what we have been trying to do in both projects. But we are getting ahead of ourselves. Before discussing the outcomes of the road testing, we need to outline the background to the original benchmarks and audit tools.

Why the benchmarks and audit tools were developed

The rationale behind the development of both sets of tools was similar. The Yorkshire and the Humber project was initiated by the Churches Regional Commission which felt that, while community involvement appeared to be at the core of many government policies and programmes, in practice it was often little more than rhetoric.

"It has been disappointingly inconsistent, undemocratic and poorly resourced. On the other hand, when it does happen well, good practice is often not broadcast as far as it should and lessons are not learned. Either way, the lesson has been that community involvement is not being consistently measured to help practitioners who want to do it better, communities who want it to happen better, and regulators and funders who want to know whether it is happening and, if not, why not, and how it can be improved."

In 1998 the Commission approached the Yorkshire Forward Regional Development Agency (RDA), with a view to developing and implementing a set of benchmarks that could help to make participation a reality in regeneration schemes. Yorkshire Forward agreed to fund and support this initiative, believing that the benchmarks would "help to develop understanding of community participation by all partners and provide the basis for the development and review of more effective community participation strategies". Mandy Wilson and Pete Wilde of the COGS Consultancy were commissioned to develop the benchmarks with the active involvement of community members from a range of regeneration areas across the region. At more or less the same time, another piece of work was being developed by Danny Burns and Marilyn Taylor. This work was underpinned by a similar analysis. Danny and Marilyn felt that too many institutions were allowed to get away with producing strategies that appeared to offer community participation but which turned out to be meaningless in reality; that not enough attention was paid to the capacity that institutions needed to develop in order to support sustainable participation; and that, when compared with the detail of management and finance audits (and recent public service reviews), scrutiny of community participation was woefully inadequate. The Joseph Rowntree Foundation (JRF) agreed to fund a piece of research that would enable a tool to be worked up for auditing community involvement.

JRF had also become involved in the final stages of the development of the benchmarking tool and quickly recognised connections with the work of Danny Burns and Marilyn Taylor. It could see that there was a need to assess how well both sets of materials worked in practice and to explore the possibility of bringing the two projects together. Danny Burns was asked to put together a proposal for carrying out such a

process. The resulting project was funded in part by JRF and in part by a number of other agencies, each of whom had a specific stake in the outcomes. These were Yorkshire Forward RDA (which had originally commissioned *Active partners*), the South West RDA (which wanted to use the audit tools in support of its new Market and Coastal Towns Initiative [MCTI]) and Embrace West Midlands (a voluntary sector organisation with a strategic remit for promoting black and minority ethnic [BME] involvement across the West Midlands).

The reason for road testing was straightforward. We have always believed that, although the tools have been built on detailed consultation and a great deal of expertise in, and experience of, community participation, unless they were used and tested in real situations they would remain little more than bits of paper. There is always a danger when producing tools of this sort that something is created that is theoretically strong but completely unworkable in practice. Our remit was to use the tools in a variety of different ways, in a variety of different contexts, over an extended period of time, to see what worked and what did not. This needed to involve not only an assessment of the content of the tools, but also ways in which the tools could be used.

A series of important process issues were raised right from the start.

Dependency

By helping people to think through issues with a framework you almost automatically set up a dependency which has to be worked through from day one. But successful implementation depends on flexibly responding to local circumstances.

"If you present a model, then people think that there is a straightforward way of implementing the model." (Mandy Wilson, Research Team meeting, 22 October 2002)

Complexity versus simplicity

Institutions facing an 'audit overload' were saying to us: "Make it simple", "Give us one or two indicators and leave it at that". We strongly resisted this on the grounds that it was too easy to show superficial evidence of involvement unless institutions were assessed at a high level of detail. But how could we make this a manageable process? The real issue here is that rather than simplify things so that they become easily useable but meaningless, people need routes into the complexity. This is what we hope the tools offer.

Carrots versus sticks

Is this process about carrots or sticks? Is it about self-development and peer review or inspection which carries sanctions? If the idea of the process is to hold institutions and partnerships to account, then without sanctions it can be a meaningless process. On the other hand, without owning the process the chances of anything happening may be extremely limited. This also raises the issue of whether the audit process should be *voluntary* or *compulsory*, and whether it should be externally assessed or self-assessed.

Does the process need to be facilitated?

A question that has run through this process is whether these tools can be used effectively without facilitation. Can a local group or an institution pick up one of the documents and work with it in a way which moves it forward? Can good information be gained through using these frameworks in other formats – such as questionnaires?

The two assessment frameworks in a nutshell

Before exploring the process of road testing in more detail, it may be helpful to briefly recap the two frameworks. What follows are two direct excerpts from the original reports (in tinted boxes). Readers who want more detail will need to refer to the original volumes.

Active partners *in a nutshell*

Active partners provides a framework that can be used by regeneration partnerships to develop an understanding of community participation. It helps to focus attention on what is already in place and what still needs to be achieved to maximise community participation. They can be used to raise the profile of community participation (and its role within regeneration) and to develop the understanding of community participation by all partners. The framework is based upon four important themes (dimensions) of community participation.

The four dimensions of community participation

Influence How partnerships involve communities in the 'shaping' of regeneration plans/activities and in all decision making	**Inclusivity** How partnerships ensure all groups and interests in the community can participate, and the ways in which inequality is addressed
Communication How partnerships develop effective ways of sharing information with communities and clear procedures that maximise community participation	**Capacity** How partnerships provide the resources required by communities to participate and support both local people and those from partner agencies to develop their understanding, knowledge and skills

Whilst these dimensions inter-relate, all four require careful consideration in order to develop opportunities for meaningful community participation.

Each of these four dimensions is further broken down into a number of aims to provide 12 benchmarks in total. These benchmarks describe what partnerships should be working towards. Each benchmark is accompanied by key questions for consideration.

Whilst specific consideration needs to be given to each benchmark, they are all integral elements of a coordinated community participation strategy and all need to be addressed in the development of action plans and the measuring of progress.

The benchmarks were designed to be used across the whole range of regeneration contexts but were also seen as relevant to other programmes and policies including health (Health Action Zones), children (Sure Start) and planning (Local Strategic Partnerships). The aim was to provide a framework for community participation strategies within which clear objectives and action plans could be developed for progress in relation to each benchmark. Benchmarks should inform the planning of regeneration schemes from the very start. Whether used for planning or review they should not be used as a tick-box exercise but a process in which communities themselves participate. The benchmarks can be used to compare and share experience and achievements in order to support best practice. However, any use of the benchmarks for comparing progress across schemes has to take account of the different contexts and starting points within which they are operating.

INFLUENCE

Benchmarks	Key considerations
The community is recognised and valued as an equal partner at all stages of the process	Who has had the first word in your regeneration strategy and how are community agendas reflected from day one and throughout the process? How are community members made to feel valued as equal partners?
There is meaningful community representation on all decision-making bodies from initiation	How are communities represented on decision-making groups (in addition to/instead of the bigger players such as local councillors)? How are your decision-making processes enabling communities to be heard and to influence?
All community members have the opportunity to participate	How are you supporting community networks/structures through which all communities can contribute to decision making? What are the range of opportunities eg creative/flexible approaches, through which community members can influence decisions?
Communities have access to and control over resources	In what ways do regeneration workers and decision makers make themselves accessible to community members? How is community control of resources being increased?
Evaluation of regeneration partnerships incorporates a community agenda	How are you ensuring community ownership of evaluation processes?

INCLUSIVITY

Benchmarks	Key considerations
The diversity of local communities and interests are reflected at all levels of the regeneration process	What steps are you taking to ensure that all communities can be involved with and influence regeneration strategy process and activity? What actions are you taking to ensure that representation by all partner agencies and staff composition reflect the gender balance and ethnic diversity of the geographical area?
Equal opportunities policies are in place and implemented	What support and training is offered to the development of equal opportunities policies and anti-discriminatory practice? How are you monitoring and reviewing practice in relation to equal opportunities?
Unpaid workers/volunteer activists are valued	How do you support and resource unpaid workers and voluntary activists? What opportunities do you provide for their personal development and career progression?

COMMUNICATION

Benchmarks
A two-way information strategy is developed and implemented

Key considerations
How do you ensure that information is clear and accessible and reaches all communities in time for it to be acted upon?

How are those involved in regeneration informed about the communities with whom they are working?

Benchmarks
Programme and project procedures are clear and accessible

Key considerations
What steps are you taking to ensure that scheme procedures facilitate community participation rather than act as a barrier?

CAPACITY

Benchmarks
Communities are resourced to participate

Key considerations
What resources are provided for the development of community-led networks and community groups?

What support is provided for community members and community representatives?

What strategy is in place to support community-led sustainability?

Benchmarks
Understanding, knowledge and skills are developed to support partnership working

Key considerations
How are you ensuring that all partners (including senior people from the public and private sectors), develop the understanding, knowledge and skills to work in partnership and engage with communities?

What training is provided and who is participating in both the delivery and learning?

The Community participation audit *in a nutshell*

The following extract (in shaded boxes) from the introduction to *Auditing community participation* outlines the broad framework and the key issues that were important to their construction.

The design of the audit tools needed to address four key questions:

- What to measure?
- How to measure it?
- What the measures offer to those engaged in partnerships?
- Who should do the measuring?

Building on the earlier discussion, we were looking for something that would ask simple but meaningful questions, that would be easy to use, that would be useful and relevant to all the stakeholders and that would have credibility.

What to measure

The audit tools are grouped under five headings. The initial section is designed to establish the context within which participation is being introduced.

The next three sections ask what needs to be in place for community participation to be effective. These questions are based on the three problem areas that we identified ... and aim to establish whether adequate systems and processes are in place to ensure that the participation can be achieved.

They cover:

- The participation strategies adopted by partnerships and the 'rules of the game'.
- The structure, culture and management of partners' own organisations and the extent to which these allow them to engage with and respond to communities (the 'capacity' within partners).
- The organisational capacity within communities.

These three areas form the core of the audit tools. They are followed by a short section on outcomes.

In each area, there are a small number of questions that the audit needs to address. Each question is followed by a short paragraph explaining why it is important and stating the indicator that the response would provide.

1 Mapping the history and pattern of participation

Key question	Indicator
A What is the range and level of local community activity?	Partners have a clear picture of the range and levels of community participation which already exist.
B What communities are there within the localities covered by the partnership?	Partners have a clear picture of the different communities that may wish to participate.
C What local barriers are there to participation?	Partners are aware of the barriers to participation and have considered how they might be addressed.

2 The quality of participation strategies adopted by partners and partnerships

Key question	Indicator
1a Who or what has determined the rules of the partnership?	Local communities are involved as equal partners in setting the rules and agendas for the partnership.
1b What is the balance of power within the partnership?	Communities have as much power and influence as other key stakeholders.

2a Where in the process are communities involved?	Communities are involved in all aspects of the participation process.
2b How much influence/control do communities have?	Communities are given the opportunity to have effective influence and control.
3a What investment is made in developing and sustaining community participation?	Partnerships invest significant time, money and resources in participation.
3b How strong is the leadership within partnerships and partner organisations?	There is long-term, committed and skilled leadership for participation within the partnership and partner organisations.
4 Does the community participation strategy allow for a variety of 'ways in'?	(a) A variety of different approaches to participation are being tried. (b) Attention is paid to strengthening all forms of community participation.

3 The capacity within partner organisations to support community participation

Key question	Indicator
5 Can decisions be taken at neighbourhood level?	Decisions can be taken at a level that local communities can influence.
6 Do decision-making structures systems allow for local diversity?	Neighbourhoods/localities can be different from one another.
7 Are services 'joined up'?	Partner organisations can deliver integrated solutions to problems.
8 Are service structures compatible with community participation?	Service structures, boundaries and timetables are compatible with neighbourhood and community structures, boundaries and timetables.

4 The capacity within communities to participate effectively

Key question	Indicator
9 How accessible are local meetings?	Local community groups are accessible to potential members.
10 Are community groups able to run in an effective and inclusive way?	Local groups work in an effective, open and inclusive way.
11 How do groups ensure that their representatives are accountable?	Representatives are accountable and have the power to make decisions.

5 Impact assessments

Key question	Indicator
12 How effective is participatory decision making?	(a) Issues of importance to the community get onto agendas. (b) Decisions made by the community are implemented.
13 What are the outcomes of participation?	Outcomes result from participation that would not have happened if participation had not occurred.
14 Who benefits from participation?	(a) Opportunities are provided for all sections of the community to participate. (b) Participation benefits all sections of the community

There are many more issues that could be audited under each heading, but it is important to start with a process that is manageable. The ... tools are intended as a starting point only, drawing attention to some of the key issues. The tools will be piloted and need to be customised for local use, drawing on the ideas and priorities of local communities and other partners.

How to measure it

For each of these questions, there is a 'tool' or 'appraisal exercise'. There are three main types of audit tool:

1. Baseline mapping exercises to establish the context within which participation is being introduced.
2. Checklists of:
   - activities or approaches that contribute to effective community involvement;
   - questions that need to be asked if community involvement is to be effective.
3. Scales to help stakeholders think through the quality and extent of the participation activities that they are putting in place.

Some of the questions require **statements of fact**, which can be used to make assessments of participation at different points in the development of a partnership, but many (especially the checklists and scales) require **subjective judgements**, because they are difficult to measure in any objective way. These judgements may vary between partners and communities.

A fourth kind of tool, which applies only to outcomes, is a 'decision trail' to track:

- how and whether selected items raised by communities get on to the decision-making agenda;
- how these items are eventually decided – and by whom;
- how the decision was reported back to the various partner organisations and communities;
- what happened to the decision en route to implementation;
- if and how it was implemented and by whom;
- how it was monitored.

The decision trail can be used in two ways. It can start with an item that a local community puts on the partnership agenda which can be tracked through the decision-making process to see whether it is implemented or blocked. Using a decision trail would be like putting dye in the system and seeing where it flows through and where it gets blocked. Alternatively, the decision trail can start with a decision that has clearly come out of the partnership and track[ed] back to where it came from. This is equally important: it is important for partners to be prepared to ditch cherished top-down plans that local communities do not see as a priority; it is also important that communities as well as partners are creating the agenda for partnership.

What the measures offer

The tools are designed to:

- identify the elements that make for effective partnership with communities – the issues that agencies and communities in partnerships need to think about;
- identify the options that are available for effective community participation;
- identify where there is room for improvement;
- identify where there is already good practice to build on;
- offer external validation.

They give participants in [a] partnership some criteria with which to engage in debate, but they can be customised to the local situation. Their purpose is to act as an aid to analysis, debate and learning within the partnership. The intention is that they should give partnerships the tools to:

- develop a strategy;
- assess their progress over time;
- compare different experiences and perceptions within the partnership;
- learn together about what works and what does not;
- benchmark against other partnerships.

For example, those tools that require subjective judgements provide an opportunity to compare and contrast the perceptions of different stakeholders. Thus, asking 'What is the balance of power within the partnership?' will show whether different stakeholders have different views on this subject. It will also provide the basis for discussion about the evidence on which these views are based. The extent to which different stakeholders make different judgements may change over time, with more agreement as and when power is shared more widely....

What we did in the three pilot areas

The pilots in Yorkshire and the Humber and the South West were based on long-term engagement with communities and regeneration schemes. The work in the West Midlands was based largely on a pilot survey.

Yorkshire Forward and the benchmarking process

Since the publication of *Active partners*, the benchmarking tool has been widely accepted as a region-wide vehicle for developing, implementing and reviewing community participation strategies. Yorkshire Forward now requires Single Regeneration Budget (SRB) schemes to report on community participation action plans and progress using the tool; the government office for the region has suggested the use of *Active partners* by New Deal for Communities and other regeneration programmes; and the Regional Forum, which acts as a voice for the voluntary and community sectors, has actively promoted the benchmarks. This means that they have both a regional profile and a high level of formal institutional support.

The aims of the road-testing process were many. As well as assessing the benchmarks themselves, it was also important to evaluate their application and impact:

- how well could they assess the level and quality of community involvement in regeneration;

	South West	Yorkshire and the Humber	West Midlands
Start	January 2001	November 2000	May 2001
End	April 2002	January 2002	April 2002
Focus of research	Market towns (rural)	SRB partnerships and schemes (urban and rural)	Regeneration partnerships (local and strategic). Focus on BME communities
Role of researcher(s)	Action-based research and strategic intervention	Facilitating schemes and communities to apply the *Active partners* framework and critically review the benchmarks and their implementation	Observing regeneration board meetings, analysing interview and survey material
Number of localities	Detailed work in 3 localities (towns) and extensive work with the strategic partnership	Work across Yorkshire and the Humber	Work across 4 regeneration partnerships
Tools	*Community participation audit*	*Active partners*	Use of both tools
Degree of compulsion	Voluntary	Involvement in this research voluntary but application of benchmarks by SRB schemes an RDA requirement	Voluntary
Where project is embedded	RDA	RDA	Embrace West Midlands (a strategic voluntary organisation)

- what was their impact on the sharing of good practice within and between partnerships;
- how well could they encourage partnerships and other organisations to identify and remedy bad practice;
- to what extent could they encourage a culture change towards community participation in regeneration partnerships, and in individual partner agencies;
- how could the benchmarks themselves and the process of assessment be adapted and applied to different regeneration programmes and contexts.

COGS supported the application of the benchmarks in a variety of ways. First, they provided induction workshops for regeneration schemes, RDA scheme managers and communities; second, they worked with selected schemes to develop processes through which they could use the benchmarks to begin to review their own community participation strategies; and third, they collected information about the range of ways in which the benchmarking tool has been applied by partnerships, schemes projects and communities. This work involved:

- holding eight sub-regional workshops for SRB scheme representatives (totalling 130 participants);
- holding four sub-regional workshops for community members (70 participants);
- holding a workshop for Yorkshire Forward project managers;
- visiting a range of regeneration schemes and partnerships across the region (nine visited);
- providing ongoing support to four contrasting 'case study' schemes from across the region;
- producing additional guidance notes both for schemes and for community members;
- carrying out two postal questionnaires to all schemes and some community members in the region;
- carrying out telephone interviews with nine SRB schemes;
- hosting and facilitating a region-wide conference for community members (70 participants);
- hosting and facilitating a region-wide conference for officers, workers and management board members from SRB schemes and other regeneration programmes (85 participants).

Detailed case studies were carried out in three areas. Following an open invitation to all SRB 6 schemes in the region, nine schemes expressed an interest and four were chosen on the basis of their difference – differing geographical locations, starting points, aims and approaches: Resurgo in North Lincolnshire, Community North Forum in Sheffield, and Action Halifax and Developing Futures for Community and Agricultural Regeneration in North Yorkshire; all expressed enthusiasm for the project. Each scheme was offered up to 10 days' support. A Regional Reference Group (made up of community and voluntary group members, representatives from Yorkshire Forward, the government office for the region, the Churches Regional Commission, SRB schemes, the Regional Forum, the Children's Society and JRF) guided the road-testing process.

In December 2000, a number of workshops, aimed at people working with SRB schemes and partnerships were held across the region. These highlighted a variety of approaches to using the benchmarking tool – from developing action plans against the indicators, as an evaluation tool for a mid-term review, to quarterly evaluations. The following examples illustrate how schemes and communities tried to get the ball rolling:

- In North Lincolnshire a paper was produced for the SRB board with the intention of setting up a community representation advisory group and a half-day workshop to collect baseline data for the group to consider in developing a strategy.
- In Withernsea and Holderness, £7,000 was budgeted into the delivery plan for support and measurement, including 'Active partners compliance' plus a part-time projects and partnerships officer to help people through the SRB process. A workshop was held to begin to establish the baseline position.
- In Sheffield, one scheme carried out a baseline audit relating to the benchmarks, and some community-based events and conferences have used the benchmarking tool to focus their discussions around enhancing community participation.
- In Ripon, the terms of reference for development groups were reviewed, partly with reference to the community participation dimension of inclusivity. A paper focusing on community participation was produced for executive approval, together with a timetable.

A scheme officer carried out an initial review against the benchmarks and set up a working group.

The South West Market and Coastal Towns Initiative and the audit process

The MCTI programme was instigated by the newly formed South West RDA (SWRDA) and its partner agencies in 2001. Its purpose was to promote regeneration rooted in the community. Although £37 million had been allocated to the programme, instead of competitive bidding for a limited pot of money (SRB style), representatives of a range of agencies with power to allocate their mainstream money or lever money in, would form a 'brokering table' and respond to communities' well-thought-out plans by finding ways to help. Similarly, rather than promote short-term funding, the aim of this project was to encourage longer-term vision (20 years). The Civic Trust was employed to explain and promote the initiative and to work with (originally seven, eventually nine) pilot towns. An officer of the Development Trust Association was seconded to the initiative to provide support and administration to the development worker. As in Yorkshire, the relationship of the audit tools to the initiative was multi-faceted. The research team was offered an opportunity to test out the tools within this initiative *and* asked to evaluate the pilot through the process. Along the way, the team would also take a developmental role in relation to both local and strategic groups. The role of the researcher was to:

- assess how well the objectives of the initiative that related to community participation were being met;
- engage in the initiative as active participants and use the audit tools to facilitate discussion at a variety of levels;
- put forward constructive proposals emerging from the audit.

Testing the audit tools was seen as an integral part of this process. Of the nine areas that had been chosen for the pilot stage of the Market and Coastal Town project, the team decided to work closely with three of these: Minehead in Somerset, Melksham in Wiltshire and a conglomeration of small towns referred to as 'Towns touching the Tamar', an area which was partly in Devon, partly in Cornwall. The plan was to visit, on a regular basis, the groups who

were organising the work in these three places and carry out parts of the audit with them. Direct work with participants in the programme involved the following:

- 21 visits to the local areas, of which 17 were public meetings or meetings of the local planning group;
- 10 full-scale interviews with members of the Regional Management Group;
- attendance at all meetings of the Regional Management Group, Strategy Group and Executive (the key strategic decision-making bodies for the initiative);
- 30 less formal or telephone interviews with local officers and activists, officers of the Civic Trust and Countryside Agency (both organisations directly involved), community development consultants and other interested parties;
- four all-day events: the formal launch of the MCTI and meeting of the Regional Reference Group; two feedback days for the nine pilot towns; and the first annual conference of the MCTI, which included two workshops using the audit tools.

Black and minority ethnic communities in the West Midlands

The West Midlands part of the project involved working alongside Embrace West Midlands, a voluntary organisation that promotes the strategic interests of black and minority ethnic (BME) communities across the West Midlands. The idea of the research was to see whether either or both of the tools could be used to support the development of participation strategies for BME communities. The original intention of the research team was to develop an action research strategy with a number of regeneration partnerships. It proved difficult to gain commitment from these partnerships to engage in the process. This was not entirely the fault of the partnerships. One of the problems we discovered at a fairly early stage in the process was that we were demanding of our researchers a level of multiple skills that were challenging by any standard. The reason we mention this issue here is that it is has very important implications for the work that we are describing. The problem we had within the team was mirroring a problem we found on the ground – that there are relatively few people within regeneration organisations and programmes who have the skill mix to carry out this work without effective developmental support. This means that developmental resources for community-based action research facilitators need to be seen as a priority (see Chapter 4).

As a result we took a pragmatic decision not to pursue the action research process in the West Midlands, and instead took the opportunity to test the tools using more conventional qualitative approaches. This involved: (a) sending out and analysing a series of questionnaires (one based on the benchmarks and the other based on the audit tools), and (b) carrying out and analysing detailed interviews with particular BME groups, which included:

- Small Heath Community Forum
- representatives from the Boznian and Herzegovinan communities
- SRB 4 Community Safety
- Sandwell Ethnic Minority Umbrella Forum
- Greets Green New Deal for Communities Partnership
- Black Women's Network
- Bangladeshi Youth Forum
- Asian Elderly Forum
- Midland Vietnamese Community Association.

These were chosen to ensure a diversity of communities (ethnicity, age, and extent of settlement in the UK) and to engage different kinds of regeneration partnership. We treated this as a survey pilot, which would give us insight into how the tools might be used to construct a full-scale survey, and what issues we needed to address to attune the assessment process to BME issues. In the event, some significant differences between the tools were highlighted, and the importance of collecting comparative information over time from different stakeholders was clearly illustrated.

2

The content of the audit tools and the benchmarks

What can the tools be used for?

Since the assessment frameworks were first conceived, we were aware that they would have multiple uses. The road testing re-enforced that view and from our work we can discern at least 10 different ways in which they have been used.

- **Opening up dialogues which can lead to genuine partnership working.** Both of the tools were designed to provide a framework for dialogue, debate and development rather than simply a set of indicators by which to measure effectiveness. The tools have helped break down myths that people have about different sectors. They have also helped to open up dialogues between stakeholders with very different perspectives.
- **A simple vehicle for raising awareness about community participation.** The very fact of getting people to talk about the issues highlights their importance. They have also helped to develop a recognition of the complexity of community participation and to acknowledge that participation takes time to develop.

  "We really see the value of a year zero from the community development perspective ... community participation needs to be built into schemes even before bids are compiled, as it should be integral to development." (SRB officer)

- **Aiding transparency.** Within a regeneration context, there can be conflicts of interest. Often these are hidden, especially when members of partnership boards wear many hats.
- **Strategy development.** Both of the tools have been used in the process of strategy

development. The benchmarks provide a strategic framework for developing a community participation strategy. The audit tools offer a way of putting flesh on the bones of the strategy. Both provide reminders of the key issues that need to be thought through and taken into account. At a strategic level, outcomes of the process had a significant influence on the direction of the MCTI.

- **A resource for holding partnerships and other agencies to account.** The tools give communities something tangible with which to hold institutions to account and a basis on which to demand involvement and institutional change.
- **Assessment.** Funding bids can be assessed according to the extent to which bidders take community participation seriously, and have built it into their process. As Local Strategic Partnerships develop, the tools might prove to be of direct use to accreditors. The Audit Commission has agreed a basket of indicators for community participation based on *Auditing community participation*. If used in a way which builds on the lessons of this road-testing process, they could have a powerful role in assessment across a wide range of initiatives.
- **Measuring progress.** The tools offer a way for people to check the 'distance they have travelled' and, where it is helpful, to compare their own progress with that of others. The knowledge gained from this process can be used both by those managing the initiative centrally and community partners to help them understand their experience. This is the closest to the straight audit concept. Benchmarking is often understood as a procedure through which standards are set, and progress is assessed in comparison with work of a similar nature elsewhere. However,

the context of this work is so varied that comparison alone is not appropriate. Progress will depend on the starting point of the group/organisation and the context in which they are working. The benchmarking process is therefore about measuring the distance travelled along the benchmark and the degree of learning from the process. Comparison with others can be useful for sharing and developing good practice but cannot be the sole basis for judgement.

- **Capacity building.** As a medium for public and private sector capacity building and educating people in statutory agencies, they promote understanding and awareness of the regeneration process and identify developmental needs for community involvement.
- **Initiating evaluation.** The tools presume a continuous evaluation and monitoring process, and help it to develop.
- **Making changes.** The tools have helped to facilitate the change process. By ringing alarm bells and 'unblocking sticking points', they can force new ideas and provide an outline for action. They help to question methods of working and whether community participation really happens.

The road tests highlighted the need to use the tools *both* for assessment *and* to catalyse change and development. This developmental role is particularly crucial in the early stages of an initiative.

What did the tools achieve during the pilot phase?

In Yorkshire and the Humber we can point to a number of specific effects of the benchmarks. According to the Yorkshire project team:

"It has led groups to be self-reflective. It has encouraged a challenge to what is meant by consultation and different methods of consultation are being tried. It has also led groups to questioning the degree to which they are inclusive. Within partner organisations, some scheme officers have seen it as a useful tool to begin to 'shift' (even if very slowly), the culture of partner organisations." (Draft report on the Yorkshire and the Humber road test, May 2002)

There are some good examples of the ways in which the tools were used directly to establish frameworks for participation:

- In Dewsbury, where *Active partners* was introduced towards the end of a scheme's life, the benchmarks were used to demonstrate what had been achieved in the area in order to (successfully) access future funding. Officers were keen to link into existing strategic planning processes rather than viewing it as an additional piece of work.
- In South Sheffield, the 'dimensions of community participation' formed the workshop themes at a conference to develop an emerging new community partnership.
- In Hornsea, where *Active partners* was seen as providing guidelines for practice, it helped to move the regeneration process forward and more people got involved.
- In Halifax, the benchmarks influenced the development of an 'Information and Involvement Strategy'.

A number of practical exercises were carried out as a result of the benchmarks:

- In Rotherham there was a mapping of all SRB projects to identify the extent of young people's involvement, and an officers' working group is looking at the benchmarks at the partnership level.
- In one Sheffield scheme, there was an attempt to employ a community partnership worker to facilitate the process with 'hard-to-reach' groups.

In some cases there was a direct effect on representation. "It led to the creation of community reps on programme delivery groups." There are also some examples of community representatives using the benchmarks to back them up when asserting their views, and several projects and schemes have talked of using the benchmarks to involve communities themselves in developing a community participation strategy. In other situations, however, there is little evidence that the rhetoric is embedded into working practices and it is difficult to ascertain what is and is not making any real difference. Sometimes, there are different perspectives about whether or not schemes are successfully implementing the benchmarks and there are examples of community members refuting the stated 'achievements' of schemes. One example is a partnership which promotes itself as effectively involving the community – but community members stress that while there is voluntary sector involvement, there is little community representation at the strategic level; and that despite plans for devolving regeneration budgets, no mechanism has been developed. In these contexts the tools should be used to prevent lip service.

In the South West MCTI, the most tangible impacts of the Participation Audit were (a) changes to processes and procedures at the strategic level; and (b) supporting towns to articulate their needs to the strategic level.

The following observations from the action research team in the South West give a flavour to this.

Right from the start the team was welcomed into the regional management group (RMG) and treated as wholly equal. Danny Burns and Frances Heywood were both invited to actively engage in the management of the whole partnership initiative. The officers of the various agencies who have attended the RMG most consistently and who have repeatedly shown their enthusiasm for the new approach have also been willing to listen to reports about the effectiveness of the programme and to act on them.

Time was allocated to use the audit tools with this group. In particular, the exercise about where power lay revealed a completely different list of players from those listed by the community groups.

The meetings form which was added to the audit tools seems to have been useful in improving the running of RMG meetings.

Individual meetings between the researcher and members of the RMG, to use parts of the audit tool, also revealed the lack of direct experience of community participation of the members of the RMG. This was true even of the Rural Community Council representative who was seen by the other RMG members as representing 'communities'. He was conscious of this and rejected it as

inappropriate. The interviews show the need for solid training of the senior agency partners in issues of community development and participation.

Also, once again, simple factual information emerged. One senior officer, for instance, said he had not realised that he was allowed to put items on to the RMG agenda.

At its most simple level, the audit tools helped to clarify the different roles of different agencies. In the South West, even one of the most dynamic and well-informed groups said it had no idea what the Regional Assembly was or did. At one meeting of the Regional Management Group (RMG) for the initiative, it also became clear that many of these senior agency officers did not understand the status of the regional Housing Corporation and the fact that it did not directly manage housing associations in the region, most of which are themselves national bodies. This was important because The Housing Corporation representative had been seen as bringing resources to the brokering table, and this was not exactly the case. The boxed examples below illustrate some practical changes which resulted directly from work with the pilot towns in the South West (as a result of the willingness of programme managers to respond to problems). These examples opposite are illustrative of the developmental impact that tools of this sort can have.

Problem	'One-size-fits-all' approach fails to allow for towns where regeneration initiatives are already underway.
Response	Executive agreed that a more varied approach will be used in the next phase. The meeting of the nine towns in May 2002 confirmed a change in perceptions.
Problem	Outside consultants may not be the best way of using funding: need to be able to use local talent.
Response	Executive agreed that local groups could apply to join list of consultants, and some have already done so.
Problem	Promise of less bureaucracy has not been kept. Forms of 4-5 pages just for launch event, 26 pages for projects.
Response	Hard work behind the scenes by the RDA meant simplification of access to initial funding.
Problem	Too many outsiders trying to help in the running of the group in Minehead.
Response	All the agencies agreed to stay away while they got themselves sorted as a group.
Suggestion	There should be a community representative on the Strategic Management Group.
Response	This was agreed, in principle, at a RMG meeting.

What part of the tools should be used when?

The two assessment frameworks came to different conclusions about the process of implementation. From the start, *Auditing community participation* was explicit about the sequence in which the audit should be carried out. It was envisaged as a cyclical process, which started with mapping the history and pattern of participation; and then in turn looked at the quality of participation strategies adopted by the partners and partnerships; the capacity of partner organisations to support community participation; and the capacity within communities to participate effectively. It was envisaged that at the end of the process the impacts would be assessed and this would lead to a round of action planning and new actions. The cycle would then begin again.

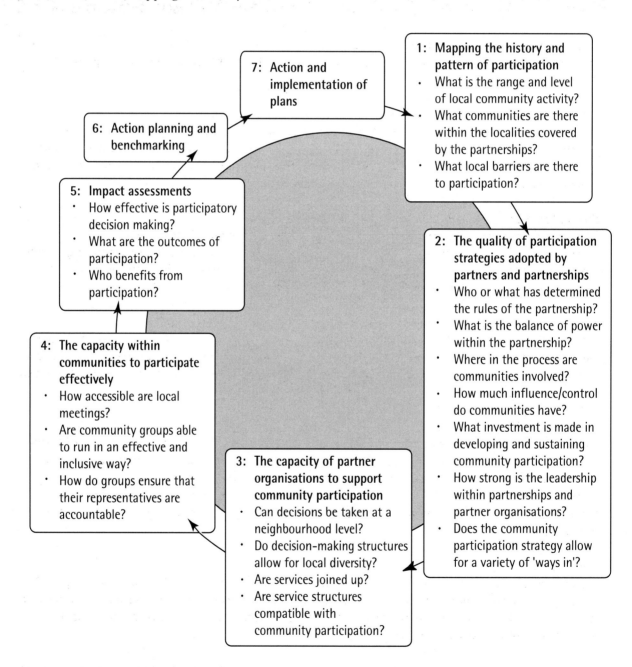

7: Action and implementation of plans

6: Action planning and benchmarking

5: Impact assessments
- How effective is participatory decision making?
- What are the outcomes of participation?
- Who benefits from participation?

4: The capacity within communities to participate effectively
- How accessible are local meetings?
- Are community groups able to run in an effective and inclusive way?
- How do groups ensure that their representatives are accountable?

3: The capacity of partner organisations to support community participation
- Can decisions be taken at a neighbourhood level?
- Do decision-making structures allow for local diversity?
- Are services joined up?
- Are service structures compatible with community participation?

1: Mapping the history and pattern of participation
- What is the range and level of local community activity?
- What communities are there within the localities covered by the partnerships?
- What local barriers are there to participation?

2: The quality of participation strategies adopted by partners and partnerships
- Who or what has determined the rules of the partnership?
- What is the balance of power within the partnership?
- Where in the process are communities involved?
- How much influence/control do communities have?
- What investment is made in developing and sustaining community participation?
- How strong is the leadership within partnerships and partner organisations?
- Does the community participation strategy allow for a variety of 'ways in'?

Following the South West road test, however, the team concluded that in most instances the audit tools could not easily be used in such a linear fashion – particularly where groups have only a small amount of time to devote to the process. In Yorkshire, on the other hand, while the team started off with a framework which could be applied pragmatically, the road-testing process led to a greater clarity about what an implementation cycle might look like. They developed the following framework.

Five steps to considering and improving community participation

Step 1: Developing a shared understanding of community participation
Communities are made up of people with a variety of interests and identities. It is therefore important to share some understanding of:

- the benefits of community participation – why it is important;
- who the 'community' is – that is, the different groups and interests that make up the community, such as distinct neighbourhoods, faith groups, women and men, disabled and non-disabled people, age groups etc;
- the key dimensions of community participation – influence, inclusivity, communication and capacity, and what they mean to different people.

Step 2: Establishing the current position
A baseline position can be ascertained by identifying where your community is now in relation to the benchmarks. The key considerations attached to each benchmark should help you to focus on the significant questions. Taking each one in turn, you could look at what has been achieved – this is an opportunity to recognise and celebrate achievement – as well as where you might be facing difficulties.

Step 3: Identifying issues and needs to be addressed
Establishing the current position should help to highlight issues that need to be addressed. It is particularly important that you gather the views of the different interests represented within your community to ensure that all perspectives are shared. You can also begin to identify the different activities that will help to develop greater and more meaningful community participation.

Step 4: Agreeing an action plan
Try to set yourselves a target for at least one benchmark from all four dimensions of community participation to ensure that there is a holistic approach to community participation. It is important to be realistic about what is achievable within any given timescale and the level of resources available. You will probably need to agree priorities and identify other groups and agencies that will lend their support. You may find the examples of practice and the indicators of achievement, which are outlined for each benchmark in *Active partners*, as useful 'prompts'.

Step 5: Reviewing progress
Community participation strategies should be reviewed in the light of progress made and outstanding needs. This is not just about what processes and procedures are in place, but how effective these are. For example, in relation to the benchmark 'There is meaningful community representation on all decision-making bodies', a review may involve an assessment of:

- numbers of community members involved, the ratio of community representatives to other stakeholders on partnership boards and on other decision-making bodies/forums;
- what has worked and not worked in terms of community influence, the extent to which different community interests and agendas have been reflected and represented in decision-making processes;
- the degree to which a wide range of community groups 'feel' there is a democratic process.

Assessment exercises, techniques and processes

Yorkshire and the Humber

The *Active partners* report, unlike *Auditing community participation*, did not include many practical exercises and techniques. However, as part of the road-testing project, a number of participatory techniques were developed, adapted or borrowed in order to facilitate application of the benchmarks. The 'What communities are there within the localities covered by the partnership' exercise from the audit tools proved to be a useful exercise to undertake before looking at the benchmarks in order to consider the overall community context in which regeneration activities were taking place. An adaptation of this exercise was also developed for logging and building up a picture of: communities; community groups and organisations; community networks; external agencies delivering services in the community; and partnerships delivering regeneration activities. The exercise was useful not only for mapping but also for raising awareness about existing routes (or lack of them) for communication about, and influence over, regeneration by different communities.

Generally, the most useful part of *Active partners* in helping people to apply the benchmarks was the 'key considerations'. These are a set of 'open-ended' questions, which help people both to understand what each benchmark is focusing on and to explore their own practice in relation to that benchmark. Answers to the questions often identified different perspectives on what had been achieved and/or what could be done to progress further.

Two exercises were developed to help schemes and partnerships think about their practice in relation to the benchmarks. These were 'benchmark speedos' and 'steps and barriers'. Benchmark speedos provide a very quick gauge of views about performance against the benchmarks. A3-sized speedometer dials running from 0-100 were produced for each of the 12 benchmarks, with the aim of each benchmark clearly displayed under the speedo. Speedos were used in a variety of situations, including community events and workshops involving those directly managing regeneration activities. Participants were asked to individually 'score' their regeneration partnership/scheme in relation to each benchmark by drawing a speedo indicator on the dial anywhere between 0 ('not doing anything to achieve aim') to 100 ('fully achieved aim'). Participants were then asked how they could 'gather speed' – what kinds of action would be needed to improve the current situation, or make the current situation sustainable. This exercise provided a very quick route to identifying areas for further dialogue and discussion. It flagged up both where there was consensus either about a high level of achievement (cause for celebration) or lower level of achievement (cause for discussing what steps to take to further progress), and where different perspectives and views needed to be the focus for further dialogue and debate. An alternative to speedos was a benchmark scoresheet, which used the same principle as the speedos, scoring performance against each benchmark on a scale of 1-5. This was more anonymous than the speedo exercise and could be sent out to groups and individuals. It also included space for comments and suggested actions in relation to each benchmark.

The 'steps and barriers' exercise involved displaying each of the 12 benchmarks on separate flip charts, with the key considerations also displayed to help people's thinking. Both the benchmarks and key considerations were sometimes slightly reworded to relate them to the specific context they were being applied to. Alongside each flip chart, two sets of symbols were provided – feet (for steps) and walls (for barriers). Participants were asked to think about each benchmark in turn and to log their own views about:

1. what the regeneration scheme in question had already achieved in relation to the benchmark (written on to feet and placed on the flipchart); and
2. what barriers – difficulties and issues – still needed to be addressed (written on to walls). This proved an effective way of sharing more detailed views than the speedo exercise. One way of building on this initial sharing was to then work in four groups focusing on the four dimensions of the benchmarks to consider further steps that could be taken to address the identified 'walls' and begin to develop proposals for a future action plan.

Other participatory exercises were developed to provide a process for moving from outline proposals for progressing community participation strategies to developing clear measurable objectives and then for prioritising these objectives. The more detailed advice and guidance provided in *Active partners* (related to specific benchmarks) was often useful in the development process strategy and also in considering how the progress of such a strategy could be measured. It was important that these exercises enabled those using the benchmarks to move fairly quickly to identifying potential future action. Although they were initially conducted with the various stakeholders already involved in decision-making structures, they also provided creative techniques for gathering the views and ideas from the wider community. The development and demonstration of such exercises became an important element of the action research, following initial findings that many schemes were struggling to find ways of engaging people in the benchmarking process.

The South West

Having determined that a tight sequential structure would not work for the audit tools, there was a great deal to be learned about what elements of the tools worked best and when. Often the facilitator had only 20 minutes to half-an-hour at a meeting, so it was important to work through just one exercise thoroughly. At other times (such as the nine towns meetings) the facilitator had a whole day and could do considerably more. She found that those parts of the audit tool that measured progress were particularly useful for meetings where a variety of individuals could do the same exercise. Exercises that demonstrated communication problems could be repeated at six-monthly intervals and regional officers charged with making the changes could be held to account. Communities which had identified differences between themselves and other areas could get in touch later to explore the reasons for those differences and so on. Some of the exercises offered an instant measurement, which was valid in itself. For example, at the meeting of the pilot towns in May 2002, a tool was used that asked participant groups to describe how much freedom and autonomy they felt their group had had within the MCTI by selecting a position on a

menu that presented different levels of choice. These choices were:

1. a uniform product (one meal for all);
2. selection of pre-set choices (you can select from a menu);
3. variations on pre-set choices (you can ask for carrots instead of peas with your meal);
4. innovation allowed, but it has to be centrally approved (local menus are approved by the centre);
5. local flexibility (people can do what they want locally but in practice they tend to conform);
6. total freedom (you can go in and ask the chef to cook you anything).

Four groups selected position '4'[1] , one participant selected position '5' and one participant selected position '6', adding "but we've been reined in". These answers were clear in themselves, and showed a high level of consistency. (These exercises can also be used as the basis for comparison when new communities join the scheme.) At the same meeting, 'speedometers' were used to measure each participant group's feelings on four different key issues: community development, officer and infrastructure support, provision of information and communication. To give some substance to some of these exercises, we discovered, for example, that, on a scale of 0-100:

- Community development support was experienced by one group as close to 70, while another felt it was at zero.
- Effective officer support was experienced at a similar range of levels, but with completely different towns giving high and low scores.
- Effective infrastructure support ranged from 20 to over 90.

The contrasting experiences here were highly informative, and opened up the question as to why towns had such different experiences – or why individuals perceived the situation differently. On the fourth issue, however, it was the consistency that was illuminating. For 'Provision of information and communication from the central management', one group gave a score of 50 while the other five all gave scores between 20 and 30. This enables those making

---

[1] One group qualified their answer by saying that it was never quite sure what the set menu was or whether variation was really allowed.

an assessment to gauge a level across the whole of the system within which they are working. These tools worked well, but it is worth noting that the outcomes of these exercises are not entirely straightforward, as people rate their decisions differently because they have different expectations – another reason why these processes need to be facilitated.

It is a common experience when using the audit tools that an exercise itself takes around 10 minutes, but the discussion that follows lasts over an hour. The audit tools exercise (Burns and Taylor, 2000, p 20) – 'Who or what has determined the rules of the partnership?' – had this effect whenever it was used. In the process of feedback, as assumptions were checked, a lot of factual information was revealed: the fact that one person present attended the RMG, which none of the others knew about ("We'll have to be polite to you now"); the view of the whole group of the RMG as being seen as wholly remote; the view expressed by one person that this group was also powerful "because nothing would happen without us". Equally major discrepancies in perceptions were identified. The exercise on power in the partnership carried out by members of the nine local towns produced completely different results to the same exercise carried out by the strategic management group. Once again this forms the basis for productive dialogue. One exercise brought out the fact that participants brought to the meetings the agenda of their own organisations – "The reason I am allowed to come is that there will be some benefit for X". These kinds of exercises are not meant for measuring or benchmarking, but more to aid reflection, the checking of assumptions and sharing of information. At this late stage we realised we should have done more of this with the RMG.

While some of the tools asked groups what they thought of outside bodies and structures, others were about the group's own performance. Exercise A (Burns and Taylor, 2000, p 12) was designed to challenge a local group to reflect on its own inclusivity. Exercise B (p 14) invited participants to list different types of community, and the answers when pooled were inevitably wider than any one person's thinking, so that the group automatically enriched itself. Exercise C (p 16) asked people to consider, among other things, which groups were not well represented and what the barriers were to their inclusion.

This should have had a challenging effect, although the researcher was surprised at how many excluded groups were still not mentioned when she used it, so it does not necessarily work without other input as well.

Exercise 10 'Are community groups able to run in an effective and inclusive way?' and exercise 11 'How do groups ensure that their representatives are accountable?' (pp 48, 50) were more challenging still. It would be a matter of judgement whether a group was strong enough to be ready for these exercises. The research certainly found that a number of the exercises depended on groups being fairly established before they could be effective.

Many of the audit tools helped users to identify problems in order to overcome them, as the examples above illustrate. But the clearest example is probably exercise 12, 'The decision trail', where an objective was selected and its progress tracked. Although this was started in three areas, progress was too slow for anything significant to be recorded. We did, however, identify a considerable number of situations where power was used behind the scenes to change or derail community-based intitiatives. If these had been captured by a decision-trail process, the evidence would have been very powerful indeed.

Finally, the question of when to use what depends on what is reasonable and for whose benefit it is done. It would, for example, have been good from the audit's point of view to have asked the local groups to map their communities, as the early stages of the audit tools suggest. This was not done in the South West because each of the towns had just completed an exercise of this kind and some were angry about being made to repeat such basic things. So, once again, the pragmatics of how to use the tools is as important as the content of the tools themselves. Which leads to an important conclusion:

"My conclusion is that the individual sections of the tool address exactly the issues that are of key importance in community-based regeneration. When used properly, and at an appropriate moment, their effect is electric. All parts of the tool that I have tried have been of value and the untried ones look as if they would be equally useful for later stages or different needs. The key problems in this pilot were not to do with the questions the tool asks, therefore, but how to find an opportunity to ask them and what to do with the answers." (Frances Heywood, South West action researcher)

This found a strong resonance in the Yorkshire and the Humber:

"Understanding [the benchmarks] is not a problem – [the problem] lies in implementation, accountability and taking things forward; we need clear guidance." (SRB scheme officer)

This is an issue that we will pick up in Chapter 3.

One thing that was quite striking is that community groups found it very easy to get to grips with the issues. We had anticipated that the exercises on leadership (question 3b, Burns and Taylor, 2000, p 28) and diversity (question 6, p 38) would present more difficulties for community participants. In fact, they clearly understood the significance of the questions and their implications and had strong views on how things stood. The people struggling with the underpinning intellectual concepts were often paid officers rather than community members.

This has important implications for capacity building.

The West Midlands

In the West Midlands, we found that the survey framework provided a good way of establishing baseline positions on key issues, and had the potential to open up important dialogues – particularly where there were responses from multiple stakeholders. We had, for example, around 15 responses from the Greets Green area of Birmingham from board members, community participants and professionals, many of whom had completely different perspectives on the issues. Capturing these differences offered an important illustration of the problem of much traditional evaluation – which is that if it is seen to come from a particular quarter (professional rather than community/a particular 'faction' within the area, and so on), then it will not be

collectively owned and will not be very useful as the starting point for a developmental process.

On an entirely practical level, the survey approach confirmed something that was beginning to emerge as an issue in the South West, which is that the exercises and tables needed to be designed differently so that they could be written on to directly. This would allow them to be photocopied, distributed to everyone, and the evidence collected.

We felt that the questionnaire approach would have been usefully enhanced by interviews using the same framework, which would have been able to probe the issues in more depth (in our research, one set of people were given questionnaires and another set were interviewed). Another way to enhance the effectiveness of this approach would be to use case studies. These would complement checklists and suggestions for good practice by demonstrating how an assessment process has been conducted, the sources of 'evidence' and actions taken following the 'assessment'.

Issues of language and presentation

While we noted earlier that there were few problems for communities in conceptually getting to grips with the tools, this should not disguise the fact that language and presentation still emerged as barriers from both road tests. In trying to provide tools to suit a wide range of unknown situations, we sometimes used abstract terms or wide generalisations that were perceived as heavy going. The size of both of the tools/reports was seen by some as daunting, and this led the researchers in the South West to work exercise by exercise and the researchers in Yorkshire to produce a four-page summary of the benchmarking tools. This was not a universal view. In Yorkshire, feedback about language was diverse, ranging from "they couldn't be any clearer" to "they are too 'jargonistic'". However, we can probably conclude in relation to both assessment frameworks that, while there is a high level of conceptual understanding by community activists, some of the terminology is offputting. An interesting comment from the West Midlands highlighted an interesting issue:

As understanding grew, so did the scope for misinterpretation, for example with regard to the proposition, 'partners have a clear picture of the range and level of community participation that already exists'. Who are the partners? Does this include staff? Does it assume that if some know then the partnership knows? Is it confined to participation in this specific partnership programme or is its scope wider?

By the end of the audit tool road testing it was felt that it may be more often than not that tables would have to be reworded to be contextually relevant. The task of trying to write something general enough to be useable in all situations mitigated against it being useful in specific situations. A good example of this is the use of the term 'the partnership' and the need for an auditor/facilitator to be crystal clear with any group what exactly is meant when they ask, for example, 'who or what has determined the strategic agenda of the partnership?'. A local community group cannot always see the whole picture. They need to know whether you are asking about the bit they can see or the bits they do not know about! Another example was our discovery that the audit tools were biased towards an urban setting – this required us to re-present them to fit a rural situation (for example, 'councillors' have had to become 'county councillors', 'district councillors' and 'town/parish councillors', a complication not familiar to groups in large metropolitan areas). The benchmarking research identified a similar need, and in Rotherham a group of young people reworded the benchmarks to make more sense of them.

The layout of the audit tools did not prove to be user-friendly – despite a great deal of time spent in trying to make them so. Tables that ought ideally to have been on one page for photocopying carried over onto a second page and had to be retyped, and so on.

There has also been a questioning of the terms 'benchmarks' and 'audit' – either because people feel that the statements of achievement are not directly quantifiable or because they feel the terms do not sit comfortably with the process of participation. This has led us toward the term 'assessment framework'.

The work with BME communities in the West Midlands raised some important issues about language. The broader issues about creating user-friendly materials are obviously all the more important for those that do not have English as their first language. But other issues were also raised. First, it was pointed out that the audit process is not culturally attuned to the oral tradition of many BME communities.

"A BME participation toolkit would have to use concepts and visuals which are relevant to that sector of the community. The toolkit could look at integrating the 'oral tradition' of BME communities."

Another connected issue is the relatively low levels of English literacy among some of those who do not have English as a first language – which means that some people are unable to engage. Even those who have excellent spoken English (and are perhaps able to read English well) may not be able to write it well. This will inevitably mean that questionnaires will not capture as much detail as we might hope for. There is an issue of power here, because even if many people from BME communities participate in the evaluation process, this does not mean that their views will be articulated as strongly as those of others. As the MEL (2002) report pointed out:

"It is ironic that the very process of auditing community involvement appears to exclude communities."

This suggests that facilitation is very important and that the use of a variety of benchmarking techniques (such as drawing) may be helpful. More broadly, ways of capturing important messages through dialogue will be essential (see Chapter 3).

Further issues raised by the work with black and minority ethnic groups

The following issues of specific relevance to BME communities offered an important perspective on what needs to be addressed in the audit tools. Unless otherwise stated, anonymised quotes come from the pilot survey.

It was clear from our work that there are considerable assumptions made by partnerships about neighbourhoods and their constituent communities. Exercise B offered a vehicle for looking at these (Burns and Taylor, 2000, p 14).

As we have already noted, there are important issues of language relating to formal protocols. Any check on information therefore needs to focus specific attention on the formal part of the process, such as funding application forms.

"The bureaucratic nature of programmes and procedures excludes BME communities. The programme and project procedures are only clear to those who are involved in the process."

Local neighbourhood and community activities are often not considered relevant to BME communities where their social networks spread across wide geographical areas. This gives us a reason why less people from BME communities might want to be involved in decision-making committees. It also provides support for the view that an effective community participation strategy means investment in community capacity across the board, not just in decision-making forums. This is a key factor that needs to be examined in any assessment process.

This complexity also shows us why just counting numbers of people is inadequate as a means of assessment. This is strengthened by the following points:

"There are simply too few BME representatives to achieve meaningful BME representation on all decision-making bodies. This is compounded by the fact that there are currently too many decision making-bodies."

"Partnerships are still struggling with the practical difficulties of how to gain representation of the BME community, given that BME communities are not homogeneous."

It is simply not feasible for a small amount of people to be physically present at all of the relevant committees. Furthermore, even if they were able to be there they could never adequately represent their communities. Having a presence on a committee is not the same as having power. The audit process needs to be able to capture this, otherwise there is a danger that those areas that manage to get a larger number of BME representatives can claim that they are representative when they are not. One

of the strong messages that came from the West Midlands questionnaire work was that:

"There is a tendency for partnerships to rely too much on BME representatives from a limited number of BME community organisations. This is problematic, in that no one organisation can represent all of the interests of BME communities."

An area may be able to show that it engages BME people in all of its policy making, but if they all come from one or two organisations then this can represent a very distorted form of community participation.

Michael Brown, in the background to his report (MEL, 2000), highlighted some important national figures relating to regeneration: out of over 900 SRB bids over six rounds, there were only 15 successful BME-led bids, representing 1.3% of the total. The value of these BME-led SRB programmes was £21 million, representing 0.4% of the programme budget. What follows from this is that most BME bids were relatively small (less than £1 million). These were strongly concentrated in London, the West Midlands and the South East. One of the reasons for this is that BME communities do not have the infrastructure to develop successful bids. The central conclusion must be that a great deal of developmental and infrastructure support needs to go into the sector before it has the capacity to bid. Furthermore, the long lead-times needed to develop full operational capacity led to a degree of underperformance, undermining organisations' credibility with other partners. This also militates against bids that are dependent on effective partnership.

A number of very perceptive responses to the audit tool on the way in which communities are involved were elicited by the process:

"BME representation is reflected at the implementation or task group level. BME community representatives do not take an active part in decision making at the strategic level."

"Loss of confidence in the partnership process after having been 'used' as a vehicle for attracting funding but then being excluded from project management and project delivery."

25

And also where power really lies:

"Decision making was in the province of officers and elected members, few of whom are BME."

In other words, it is not just board representation that is important but also the employed decision makers within organisations. The tools have to be sensitive enough to look into areas that are not formally part of the 'democratic decision-making' arena, but which have a major influence on it, and have to be able to compare them year on year. So in the case above, next year the assessment process might want to look at whether BME representation among officers was higher. What goes on behind the scenes is crucial. Some of those who completed the survey felt that BME control over resources had improved, but that further improvement was hampered by rivalry between BME communities. This rivalry was apparent to everyone involved but it was not made explicit in the evaluation process. This is problematic because if this is what is really blocking participation then it is no use documenting all of the other things which are less significant – solely because they are manageable and can be spoken about.

Finally, we would like to underline the importance of not trying to measure like with like:

"Some issues and problems are common to all communities, rather than being specific to BME communities. Hence all communities would be voicing concerns about the project appraisal process appearing to be overly bureaucratic and with too many opportunities for delays. However, different starting points, experiences of institutional discrimination and a history of regeneration having a low impact on BME communities compound these problems such that they weigh disproportionately heavily upon BME communities." (MEL, 2002)

What needed to be added to the frameworks?

The road-testing process prompted a number of changes and additions as we went along. In response to the requests for more guidance, COGS produced two sets of guidance notes, one for community members and one for partnerships and schemes. Each set was eight sides of A4 paper. There was some commonality between the two but they were tailored to the different needs of the different audiences. For example, the set for community members included a short 'jargon buster'. Given the comments above about the understanding of professionals, it might also be appropriate to include a jargon buster for paid officers. Many people commented that the *Active partners* was too big a document: "The full report is a bit too weighty and onerous"; "It is too lengthy and impenetrable – the four-page summary is much easier". This fits with the request for a pared-down version of the original *Active partners* report, formulated more as a checklist and ideas for action:

"We perhaps need something for communities that is halfway between the full report and the four-page summary. Try to make it look as simple as it is in reality."

As we have suggested earlier, the difficulty with moving towards such an approach is that community participation is complex. Without some care, the benchmarking tool could undermine its central raison d'etre. What many people like about the benchmarks is that they are comprehensive and do not let SRB schemes off the hook. And there is always the danger of using the benchmarking tool overprescriptively without the underpinning understanding of what it is about.

In Yorkshire and the Humber there were some requests for a more accessible and flexible format (for example, an A4 ring-binder) containing loose-leaf sheets that can be updated and added to. Suggestions for contents included:

- an *Active partners* summary;
- *Active partners* guidelines;
- a bulletin updated every six months with additional guidance, ideas of good practice and 'top tips' based on experience;

- worked-up examples and detailed case studies illustrating what can be achieved (in terms of both the process and tangible outcomes);
- a more community-focused publication; "It looks too 'official'";
- a series of worksheets;
- an example of a community development post job description;
- an example of skills criteria/person specification for community participation/ partnership posts;
- clarification and explanations with regard to 'new' terminology, for example, social capital.

Sometimes the feedback was contradictory. People wanted informal publications, but they also want to feel valued, so they did not want them to be badly produced.

During the South West pilot, new tools had to be developed to pick up issues which were not being effectively addressed by the tools. These included:

- a form for recording what happened at meetings;
- a form that asked people to indicate their multiple roles in the community – the 'hats' form, as suggested by an officer in one of the pilot towns;
- a revised version of exercise 1b 'What is the balance of power within the partnership?'. On the suggestion of one of the groups, a scale of power from 1-9 was replaced with the simpler categories of 'very powerful', 'powerful' and 'not-so-powerful';
- a form for carrying out the 'decision trail' exercise (exercise 12);
- an interview schedule for members of the RMG, asking about things such as their experience of community participation and the time they have available for the initiative.

These appear in the new handbook: *Making community participation meaningful: A handbook for development and assessment*.

In general, the means of recording input and conveying it to the person who needs to see it is an issue that has to be addressed. Simple formats for collating responses are needed, so that information can be fed back to groups. Often, it was the interchange between individuals at the point when an exercise was being discussed that was really interesting and

important, rather than the words they had written down originally. The research team wrote reports on each of the South West pilot towns which were then sent to them to be corrected and verified. These documents became an important extra tool in this audit, which involved the interweaving of many sources, not just materials from the audit tools. However, this process was not immune from political sensitivity. Fear of the power of the centre meant that, in many instances, criticism of the centre had to be fed up through the meetings of the nine towns rather than from individual towns.

Integrating the two tools

In April 2002, the full research team came together to explore the possibility of integrating the two tools. We ended up literally cutting up parts of the two books and repositioning the material in them on a large piece of flip-chart paper. We had an intuition that the two could be effectively mapped onto each other, and a sense that they had strengths and weaknesses that were complementary. As Carol Ferron Smith (researcher in the West Midlands) put it:

"The audit tool is like a roadmap. And the benchmarking is like sign posts."

So our task was to coherently lay out a road system which brought these two tools together. Our reformulated framework has three inter-related elements. First, it identifies key considerations that together lay out a framework that partners need to think through. Second, it identifies indicators that relate to each of these key considerations. And third, it identifies a set of reflective questions that can be used to unpack and assess the extent to which these indicators have been achieved.

The new handbook is published as a companion volume to this: *Making community participation meaningful: A handbook for development and assessment*.

3

Application of the two tools

Access

As we pointed out earlier in this report, the key issue that we had to face up to in this research was not the content of the tools but the access that we could gain to the various groups and stakeholders in order to work with them on it. You can have the best audit process in the world but if you cannot get through the front door then you cannot achieve very much at all. There were different problems in different areas at different levels.

In the South West, access at regional management level was remarkable right from the start; the researcher was welcomed into the RMG and treated as a wholly equal member of the team. This meant fully participating in decision making about the whole future of the programme. The officers of the various agencies who attended the RMG most consistently and who repeatedly showed their enthusiasm for the new approach were willing to listen to reports about the effectiveness of the programme and to act on them. In addition to this, the researcher was allowed time to use the audit tools with this group. The meetings form which we have added to the handbook was particularly useful in improving the running of RMG meetings. There was, however, a major problem about protecting the towns the researcher was working with, which amounted to a methodological problem about what to do with the audit information once gathered. She quickly observed that grumbles from local groups might lead to them being penalised and that any information on views about the programme must be anonymised. This is why we have reported back only views gathered at meetings where a number of the pilot towns have been present.

Access within the towns was not so simple. In the South West, the researcher could go to meetings as often as she wanted: "They felt they could not say no to my attendance". However, they were far too busy wrestling with the demands of the new programme on top of their existing work (and without, for a long time, any extra resources), to take in what she was there for or willingly find any time for it. It took almost the whole length of the project to turn this around. Sometimes this meant travelling 100 miles to get a 20-minute slot in a meeting. This slowly led to the building of a relationship and the possibility of carrying out more work. As we shall see, this has a direct bearing on the issue of 'voluntary or compulsory' assessment.

Access to formal decision-making structures and access to the 'corridors of power' are two quite different things. In the context of the South West, the capacity for the audit process (and the information which was coming out of it) to feed into real change was closely linked to the relationships that the action research project coordinator and the Civic Trust officer responsible for project managing the programme had built with key players in the RDA. This in itself represents an important finding about the ways in which community participation strategies are implemented and sustained and we discuss this further in the section on implications of the action research process (page 31).

In Yorkshire and the Humber, access has to be interpreted slightly differently as the researchers had a different role. They were not themselves carrying out any assessment or audit of community participation but were facilitating the process of self-assessment. They did, however, observe some issues similar to those faced in the South West. In particular, there were many examples of schemes struggling to find the time to give sufficient (or any) attention to the benchmarking process alongside other pressing business. A key focus of the research was SRB 6 schemes, which were only just up and running at the time of the road testing and were immersed in both meeting other RDA requirements and getting their delivery mechanisms in place. It also appears that for some schemes, application of the benchmarks was a low priority because of its perceived unimportance. Many of the schemes that embarked on the benchmarking process most effectively introduced the process at a 'business' meeting to gain commitment to the process, and then delegated responsibility to a working group and organised specific workshops or away days to make further progress.

The interviews with key organisations in the West Midlands highlighted other important issues with regard to access:

- delays through being referred from one person to another when trying to make the initial approach to the partnership;
- delays making contact with the single person identified as responsible for this work (often it is only one person who leads on community involvement on behalf of the partnership);
- referral to sub-committees for action as these are deemed to be more accountable to the community since they have community representation.

Time and timing

One of the key issues that arises from these conclusions about access is the amount of time needed to do this work effectively. Within the timescale of the road testing it was not realistic to measure significant outcomes of either the audit tool or the benchmarking tool in relation to enhanced community participation. Progress has been more related to ways in which they have helped to develop understanding of community participation and awareness of what issues need to be addressed within any forward strategy. In the short term, action needs to be related to agreed priority objectives that lead to progress along at least some of the benchmarks. But it needs to be acknowledged that in the first stages, assessment will need to focus on process and infrastructure. It will probably only be possible to assess outcomes after a number of years.

Individual capacity-building outcomes can start to be identified within three to five years (although they need to be noted and recorded early on). It will probably take nearer five to 10 years to identify community social capital outcomes. This reinforces the need to see this work as a long-term process, which needs long-term commitment and investment.

In the South West, important issues were raised about when it was best to do some interactive auditing. Because of the huge pressure on the groups to perform the essential tasks of the MCTI in the first year we considered that it would be better to start assessment in year two after they had secured some initial funding. One way to make the audit more possible in the early stages would be to emphasise their use as a development resource in the early phases.

The earlier analysis of the different functions of the audit tools gives clues about the length of time needed to use the different tools. Time needed varies with function. Thus, the measuring/benchmarking aspects of some of the tools can be carried out very quickly (10 minutes each was enough for the 'speedometers' and 'menus'). Tools that are to stimulate immediate discussion or challenge may be just as quick to administer, but it is the feedback and discussion that is important and, in a group of eight to 10 people, this is likely to take 40-60 minutes. If the people doing the auditing were not travelling 150 miles to the meeting but were on hand anyway, it would be perfectly reasonable to carry out regular 10-minute audit exercises as part of a programme of feedback. Putting these thoughts together, about the problem of time and the different functions of different tools, the logical way forward would be to say that community development/support workers working with local groups would often be the right people to use these tools with the groups. They could feed replies back to a central coordinator, who could then collate and anonymise them as necessary. One of the most important issues here is that it can take the researcher a considerable period of time to fully understand what is necessary in the particular contexts within which they are working.

The issue of when meetings take place – especially when voluntary groups and statutory agencies interact – is of the greatest importance, and central to the policy of community-led projects in general, but it has not been faced or resolved. Meetings either take place in the day and exclude voluntary activists who have daytime jobs, or they take place in the evenings when officers are reluctant to come and everyone is tired and want meetings as short as possible.

The need for facilitation and expertise

One of our strongest conclusions is that the process and most of the exercises need a facilitator. This is in part because if their primary purpose is developmental then the aim of the exercises is to open up a dialogue about the issues. In the case of the benchmarks:

"The issue has not been about facilitation versus self-assessment. What the road-testing project has highlighted is the need for skilled facilitation of the self-assessment process and the fact that many partnerships and schemes either do not have people with such skills within their own workforce and membership or are not recognising the need for such facilitation. The process of involving all stakeholders in the assessment process requires an understanding of community participation, the development of creative and participative ways of gathering the experiences and views of different stakeholders and the skills to help people discuss and work through differences of perspective, understanding and ideas." (Pete Wilde)

Frances Heywood advances other arguments to support this view:

"Words will often need to be adapted to fit a particular situation so as to be really clear to all participants. Someone has to do this, and someone has to choose what will be useful. Also, the exercises where the message needs to reach central management have to have a route to get there."

The role of the facilitator as a bridge is critical:

"I became a messenger, a communicator, I saw the terrible misunderstandings, the gaps, the failings."

But the process has to involve more than facilitation. We felt that it needed to be situated within a clear action research framework so that action could result directly from the evaluation, and so that the discussions were strongly rooted in reflective practice. A good example of why this is necessary came from the South West. Here, while the concept of a brokering table had underpinned the process, people throughout the system continually slipped back into a 'grant-allocating' mentality. If a reflective exploration of this pattern had taken place earlier, some of the problems of the initiative may have been resolved earlier.

Partnerships need to ensure that skilled facilitation resources are available for:

- auditing the central group itself – to help strategic planners and senior managers develop their understanding of how to work in partnership with community partners and to identify their own problems;
- carrying out audit/benchmarking through meetings of the community partners, and feeding the findings back both to the participants and to the central managers as a way of demonstrating achievement and flagging up problems that need to be addressed;
- supporting local groups if they want the service for their own purposes. (There may be occasions when the use of an outsider would be considered desirable.)

Facilitators should be based within the region so as to be flexibly available. They will need to have the kind of policy knowledge base to do the work well (see p 33 for more details). They also need to have a direct link to a senior member of the central team, probably the officer responsible for the policy and implementation of community involvement. Equally, training and support could be offered to community activists, community development workers and community planners to familiarise them with the audit and benchmarking tools. These tools could then be added to the repertoires of these local professionals and community activists, for use when they felt they were appropriate. A website, perhaps set up by JRF, could act as a source for the tool formats and ideas from anyone working in the field. This approach would make possible the well-targeted, little-and-often approach that was not possible with a single facilitator/auditor travelling long distances.

Issues raised by the action research process

As we have strongly asserted above, the most effective way to do this work is through a facilitated process. Through the road tests we adopted two slightly different approaches loosely based on an action research model. Neither closely corresponded to a classic action research project because, although long-term relationships were established with the groups, it was rarely possible to get the kind of extended time that would have been necessary.

Action research of the benchmarks in Yorkshire and the Humber was undertaken within the context in which this set of 'tools' was developed. It had a strong 'capacity-building' flavour, focusing explicitly on the application of the benchmarking tool itself (as well as the implementation of new procedures of accountability). The team gathering information from across the region about application of the benchmarking tool (through surveys, workshops, and so on), directly facilitated understanding and application of the benchmarks (through work with case studies, training, workshops, production of further guidelines, and so on), and evaluated the benchmarking tool and its implementation. The element of action research that most closely resembled the process used with the audit tools was the work carried out with three case study SRB 6 schemes. Here it had a dual role of assessing and offering advice.

Frances Heywood described the process in the South West as follows:

"When people are told that an 'audit' of community participation is to take place, they may envisage it as: (i) like a financial audit: checking the situation at a given moment in time and making a report without interfering in any way. If it is then described as 'action research', they may envisage the task as being more like (ii): that of scientist noting the growth of plants treated in different ways and intervening with suggestions to the gardeners of more sunlight or ways of keeping off the slugs.

In practice, I have found using this audit as an action researcher is more like (iii): being a chemical catalyst, trying to note the change going on all around in the test-tube while you are in it and causing some reactions yourself. The difference is that a catalyst is supposed to be itself unchanged, while the action researcher will themselves learn and change, too."

It would have been impossible to be clear at the start about this role either to the local groups or to the regional management and other involved officers, because it evolved as the project went on. Initially, the intention was just to record the situation as in (i) or possibly (ii) above. In practice, the potential to help the MCTI succeed was too great to ignore. Frances Heywood was present at RMG meetings where information and understanding gained from the audit was needed. She was present at local meetings where she could have a productive facilitative role. The whole situation was moving too fast for action to be taken by waiting three months to make a report on situations which by then might have been very hard to retrieve.

The RMG had agreed to move this way, but through no fault of their own had not really understood it, and we think that they still expected something more clear cut: regular reports on how well they were doing in running the new initiative in a 'bottom-up' way. In the end, they have received this in the form of a final report, and we hope it will prove useful and encouraging to them.

A similar issue arose with the benchmarks – where, because the action research process itself was evolutionary, there was some lack of clarity about who should be driving the change:

"A key difficulty subsequently faced by the action researcher was that they were looked to for leadership and did on occasions take a more proactive role than initially intended to avoid any progress falling into a vacuum. This reflected the fact that the resources required to apply *Active partners* had not been thought about clearly enough. This highlights the need for people to understand the role of the researcher in the context of their work. In retrospect there should have been more discussion about this in selecting the case studies. Ideally, there needed to be an existing or established grouping within each scheme structure responsible for driving the process with the action researcher providing support." (Pete Wilde and Mandy Wilson, working draft report)

The aim of both processes was to catalyse local leadership but there was always a temptation to defer to the facilitators.

PW/MW: "The difference was the relationship to Yorkshire Forward."

DB: "So you were seen as having a bit more power. And what effect did that have?"

PW/MW: "People thought that we had the answers and that we would give it to them, and that they would then be able to satisfy Yorkshire Forward. People thought that we knew more about Yorkshire Forward than we did." (Research team meeting, 22/11/2002)

A number of other issues arose out of the engaged nature of the research process. A critical one lies in the issue of how we use our power. There is a fine line in this kind of audit/ action research between being a helpful messenger/mediator and being a talebearer or spy running between two camps, at risk of betraying confidences given in good faith. Any audit process has this element to it, but it is not always so personal and people are usually much clearer about the rules. The power that the South West researchers had in the MCTI lay in:

(1) the knowledge that was acquired from attending meetings at different levels;
(2) access to the key personnel involved in the initiative outside of formal meetings;
(3) the opportunity to influence the agenda and write papers with recommendations for the RMG;
(4) the opportunity to speak and to vote at meetings of the RMG.

"The work of Danny Burns, in conjunction with the Civic Trust officer has been key in taking the information from the audit and using it to negotiate for changes with the programme managers. Without such a structure for implementation the audit would probably not have achieved much. I consider this a very important point." (Frances Heywood)

There was, in short, a real opportunity to influence the Initiative through the audit, but it carried with it some ethical dilemmas.

On a practical note, there is a constant problem about people being present when audit tools are to be used whose presence may be inhibiting. This has happened so often that it seems fair to say it cannot always be helped. Delivering painful messages is also problematic. Some of the complications that we faced were because we had multiple roles. On the one hand, we were road testing the exercises in the *Community participation audit*. On the other hand, we were facilitating a developmental process for local groups and strategic decision makers. We were also inputting our learning into the formal evaluation of the programme. Ironically, one of the exercises that we had to develop as part of the road test was one which made transparent the multiple hats that people wear. We (as participants in the process) needed to identify our own multiple hats – some of which inevitably clashed with each other. This multi-layering, which was particularly strong in our work, will always be present to some degree but for most users of the assessment frameworks it should not involve quite so much complexity.

By engaging in an action research process, the researchers had to be explicit that they were not engaging as neutral observers. Building trust means building relationships. This can make it difficult to say some of the things that are hard to say, or to talk openly about "mistakes by individuals who had powerful positions in the initiative". One important issue to take account of is that by virtue of being an action researcher you get very close to the personalities involved and do not see things objectively. If you develop a close working relationship with people it is difficult to criticise them (even constructively!):

"I got off to a tricky start here by producing a report that was too personal." (Frances Heywood, draft report on the South West pilot)

A later reflection on the process by Frances Heywood captures the nature of the problem:

"This process of audit has been hard, both for myself and for others: we have been guinea pigs in an experimental situation. The findings of the audit have sometimes hurt other people and this process has been painful to me, although in most cases, we have eventually emerged from this process with greater understanding and good relations restored or established. The process of reflecting on the auditing process and considering the lessons from it has been very important and led to change and growth. Action research like this is more art than science. Inevitably the personality and experience of the researcher affects what is done as they must judge what tools to use, when to use them, how to feed back, when to intervene and how to handle really difficult situations. This is akin to the work the community development/support consultants are doing in the various towns, but different because the researcher is not working directly for any group and is more of an outsider. A degree of isolation is probably unavoidable, but mentoring and support for the action researcher in this process can make all the difference and should be seen as essential." (Frances Heywood, May 2002)

The process also meant understanding and engaging with the power flows that ran through the whole system. One illustration of this was Frances Heywood's role on the RMG of the MCTI. At the beginning of this process she was welcomed to every RMG meeting, but towards the end she was excluded from one meeting of the strategy group, designated for 'director level only'. In the later stages of the process it was discovered that the RDA had decided to appoint consultants to write another report on the initiative – a task the research team thought that they were already doing. This suggests that, unless the process is 'pinned down' (perhaps within a compulsory audit framework), it is just as easy to prevent access (when politically expedient) as it is to let people in (as the researchers experienced at the beginning of the process). Even within an initiative that is innovative and politically sympathetic to community-based initiatives, a vast amount of decision making still takes place in the 'corridors

of power', invisible to mainstream audit processes. We hope that the 'decision trail' exercises will help disentangle some of these issues. We may also need to look at a 'reverse' decision trail that is like organisational 'speleology'. Here, rather than looking at where proposals were blocked, we would look at how decisions came to be made. This is perhaps the most important reason why the audit process needs to be wrapped within a facilitated process. An action researcher has to use political skill and judgement about how best to convey key messages without losing all chance of influence.

At this point it is worth restating the importance of seeing the tools as a resource that can be applied in a variety of ways. In contexts such as the South West pilot, the tools may initially be better used as frameworks for developing participation than assessing it. The action research process allows these two processes to be integrated as the programme develops.

The skills that are needed to do this work

Both the benchmarks and the *Community participation audit* stress the need for the participation of communities themselves in applying the frameworks. The action research highlighted the fact that in many schemes and partnerships there is a lack of expertise in developing and facilitating the participatory processes that are integral to effective application of the assessment frameworks. The schemes that appear to be making most progress are those with dedicated community development staff (either as part of the programme administration or as separate projects). The Yorkshire and Humberside research concluded that there was a need for there to be a clear grouping within the partnership or scheme delegated with responsibility to take the lead on the benchmarking process. Some schemes have established working groups specifically for this purpose, while others have delegated an existing group with this task. The implementation of benchmarking by Yorkshire Forward has prompted some schemes to recruit an additional community participation worker with specific responsibility for coordinating and supporting the process. More generally, we have been struck by the lack of infrastructure support for community-based processes of this sort. The South West MCTI was supposedly a £37 million programme, which was being run by one administrator, less than a tenth of a senior manager's time, and the part-time support of a community-based consultant. This needs to be changed if the underpinning for this sort of work is to be properly put into place.

One of the main problems that we identified is that this work is more often than not delegated to scheme managers or project officers who have little or no understanding of community development. These officers are often the ones 'holding the baby' when the senior managers have rushed on to shiny new projects.

There is a danger that scheme managers/other officers use the documents simply as tools without understanding the processes necessary to use them effectively. This might involve managers writing convincing action plans that have no ownership from anyone else (a paper exercise); or officers setting up systems and procedures to improve participation, which are flawed either because they do not have the skills to implement them, or because they do not understand what is really needed (after all, many of these people were never employed on the basis of community development skills – their skills are often administrative or managerial).

It is also arguable that some officers have become part of the 'tick box' culture, which promotes an environment in which people have to be seen to always succeed and say 'yes, we've done that' and mitigates against exploring 'how' things are happening. There are also examples where responsibility for community participation has been passed on to an administration worker or someone else who could not be expected to be able to carry it through. Lack of community participation expertise among programme staff can create instant mistrust among communities.

Facilitators on the ground used a wide range of skills to do this work effectively; a great deal of background contextualised knowledge is needed. It was necessary, in addition to understanding the tools, principles and practice of community participation, to have knowledge of:

- the basic geography of the region, and adequate local knowledge about the towns within the region;

- the roles and responsibilities of the numerous different agencies, and the names and job descriptions of key personnel;
- the new structures of local government, as well as proper knowledge of the existing three-tier system in all the pilot towns;
- at least a basic grasp of all the other regeneration initiatives that the towns were involved in, including SRB 6 and Objective 2;
- other initiatives, such as Sure Start, that were impacting on some towns;
- key policy papers relevant to the initiative. These included the Rural White Paper, the Planning Green Paper and guidelines on Local Strategic Partnerships and Community Planning.

In addition to this knowledge they need to be multi-skilled. Our observations above should illustrate clearly the way in which action researchers in this environment need:

- well-honed political skills – enabling them to negotiate access, to work effectively with conflict, to 'smell out' hidden agendas, to skilfully play back politically charged issues to decision makers;
- good recording, observational and analytical skills – to ensure that benchmarks are recorded and the insights about process are tracked;
- excellent group work skills – because the process needs strong but sensitive facilitation, and a knowledge of action learning and action research processes;
- highly developed networking skills – this would include experience and understanding of community development practice;
- a relevant background of information – this was particularly important in a fast-moving policy environment where both events (such as the foot and mouth crisis) and changing policy (such as new guidelines on the roles and priorities of RDAs) become central to both the programmes and the individual projects.

These combinations are still not commonplace, and where they exist they are highly in demand. Within our own research team, we hit difficulties because inevitably each of the individuals had strengths and weaknesses in relation to these criteria. But we learned a lot about what was needed for this sort of work. In order to support people to develop this range of skills, agencies need to think carefully about staff development –

because few people will come to these roles with the full combination of skills required.

Recording

This project raised important questions about what needs to be recorded and how, and how information can be recorded in such a way as it is useful later as either a benchmark or as information useful for learning. The following dialogue from one of our research team days offers some interesting insights into the process. Here we explore some of the differences between the work in Yorkshire and the Humber and the work in the South West:

MW: "In the South West she was initially going in as an external auditor using the audit tools, whereas we were going in to facilitate people to self-assess. She also went in as a researcher and we're not. We wouldn't call ourselves researchers."

FH: "I was recording things all of the time to have evidence."

MW: "The process of our intervention wasn't recorded. We recorded their process."

FH: "We were trying to do three things. We were going in there to be useful to the group, and to use the tool, and to record the use of the tool. The issue of self-assessment was up front as an issue dependent on the community workers on the ground. You can't just benchmark by recording data against headline indicators."

MW: "It's about people owning what they are saying. Anyone can engage in an exercise without really engaging their minds."

FH: "Part of the methodology, because I was doing it as a researcher, came from the reports that I wrote to the towns."

PW: "When Helen did some work with individual schemes, people expected her to write it up and give them a report. She said 'no that's not my role, that's your role'."

FH: "It was necessary because [x] was denying what I was saying. If you hadn't written it up how could you have fed it back.

PW: "The only thing that we were trying to capture was how well people could use *Active partners*."

The action research has not taken place over a sufficient timescale to fully explore requirements and ideas for recording through all stages of the auditing and benchmarking process. However, we can identify key elements of recording which need to be considered.

1. Gathering and recording views and information from all stakeholders, including communities, in relation to and taking into account a scheme's/partnership's starting point in relation to the *Active partners* benchmarks. This might include: a scoring assessment of performance against each benchmark; what is in place/achieved already; key issues that need to be addressed; and ideas for future priorities/action. This provides a basis for both dialogue and the development of a forward strategy.

2. Development and recording of a forward strategy which includes key objectives, action plans, timescales and how progress will be measured.

3. Mapping exercises which show, for example, the nature of local governance in the area; the different hats that people wear and how they fit within community networks and the different communities that exist within an area.

4. Writing regular reports as a basis for ongoing discussion and validation. The researcher in the South West used this process to great effect in the local pilot areas. After extensive participant observation, she collated her impressions in a report that connected her observations to audit tools. The group was then able to discuss, correct and validate the process.

5. Recording need not be mechanistic or quantitative. Picture snapshots can be used to illustrate change. Our work with pictures was incredibly powerful. This can be integrated as

35

a mainstream way of recording changes in perceptions.

It is conceivable that these pictures had more impact on policy makers than our detailed evaluation reports.

To illustrate this last point in more detail, a very important exercise that was carried out in conjunction with the tool in the South West was based on a comparison of pictures. At a meeting of the nine pilot towns, participants were asked to draw how they experienced their relationship with whomever they perceived as the central decision makers in the initiative.

At all the meetings of the pilots in May 2002, groups were invited to draw pictures representing the relationship between themselves and the regional management of the initiative, as they had done eight months previously. Some of these appear below (the commentary is that of the authors):

Town A

There are nine seeds portrayed, exotic plants just at the stage of germination. Overhead is a black cloud that offers both nourishment in the form of £ signs dropping and potential threats. Behind the cloud, the sun is visible. The distance between the seeds (the town) and the cloud (the RMG) is a vast distance: about 10,000 miles.

Town B

A rural scene is portrayed. An RDA officer sits smiling, holding all the cards. There is an obscure forest with hurdles and steep hills representing obstacles still to overcome. There is a brokering table with empty chairs. At the bottom corner of the picture is the community (as opposed to community groups), still very marginalised. There is a hold-up signifying foot and mouth.

Town C

There is a background of political spin, Alistair Campbell and too many initiatives. The group is looking down a very long road to a very distant horizon (the RDA). But yes, there has been progress since September. And there is a small, female person with a spade. There is so much to take in, but she is smiling.

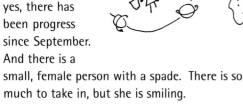

Town D

A body with no face represents the RDA, with money. It is linked to the steering group and community agents but the link is not good. There is a dashed line and a brick wall with a few bricks missing that could be crawled through. Communication is represented by a wind up-telephone and a carrier pigeon.

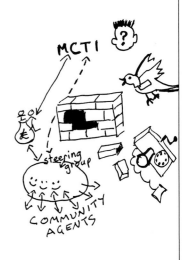

In all but one of these descriptions, the local group refers to the Regional Development Agency rather than the partnership, illustrating how great the need is to make the multi-agency nature of the initiative more evident.

In general, remoteness, powerfully presented through a variety of images, is still the main image, with poor communication, as represented by the wind-up telephone and carrier pigeon, or the brick wall with just a few gaps to crawl through, the second image, and uncertainty the third main image.

But the pictures are more positive than those drawn the previous September, where one group presented a sheet of blank paper as representing the relationship, another had dense clouds and all had great distances. This time there are a few people smiling, there are seeds sprouting and there is a house with open doors. There is hope in most of these pictures.

It is conceivable that these pictures had more impact on policy makers than our detailed evaluation reports.

Voluntary or compulsory assessment?

As we indicated in the introduction to this report, the issue of whether the assessment process should be voluntary or compulsory may have a profound effect on the success or failure of the process. There are a cluster of related questions that also need to be addressed here, such as 'Who is the assessor?' and 'Where does the authority for the process come from?'. There is something to learn here in the comparison of Yorkshire and the Humber with the South West.

In Yorkshire and the Humber, while the benchmarking process became more accepted over time, in the early stages of implementation there was a fair amount of disquiet. Two strong concerns were expressed. The first was from the SRB schemes who worried that, since the benchmarking tool was a requirement of the RDA, it was seen as yet another piece of bureaucracy (not lending itself to community participation). The second came from some communities themselves, who saw the benchmarks as a guidance tool for officers and were afraid that the scrutiny would be on them as communities rather than other partners.

Although the use of the benchmarks was not compulsory, the requirement for clear community participation strategies against which schemes had to assess their progress was compulsory – in effect, for many, this meant using the benchmarks. Following the publication of *Active partners*, Yorkshire Forward issued more stringent requirements of SRB 6 schemes (and subsequently all SRB schemes) in relation to community participation.

> It is important that all Partnerships understand the importance and demonstrate a commitment to community participation in regeneration and to that end put in place systems and strategies to support and enhance participation and effectively monitor the level and quality.... It is recommended that the benchmarks set out in *Active partners* be used.... (Yorkshire Forward, August 2000)

Despite this, the real extent of RDA support for community participation was not always clear. Many schemes and partnerships requested more clarity from the RDA, asking it to spell out the resources, support and guidance that partnerships can expect:

> "Yorkshire Forward has imposed this without adequate guidance about reporting procedures. Every other area of their work has clear outlines of what is to be provided to Yorkshire Forward, except this." (SRB scheme officer)

> "[Scheme] officers can be seen as the foes of community organisations as they have to enforce these over-the-top rules." (SRB scheme officer)

Another factor which had a significant effect on the extent to which the benchmarking was complied with was the perceived shift in the RDA's priorities. Many SRB partnerships began to question their commitment to the benchmarking tool as soon as the RDA started to stress its focus on economic as opposed to community regeneration. People commented that community participation is not "at the heart of Yorkshire Forward's beliefs" and that they were being asked to do something which had no meaning.

> "It is important that Yorkshire Forward gets across a positive message and gives clarity to its own role and obligations with regard to community participation." (community conference delegate)

It was also reported that some of Yorkshire Forward's own officers were unclear about the role of community participation and believed that SRB was not necessarily the right place for it.

In the South West, the shift of the RDA towards a stronger economic focus was also noticed by the nine pilot towns:

> "After only 18 months, just as the programme is set to expand from the original nine towns to 50 or so, there are signs of a loss of interest from the key senior officers. New projects have arisen and officers leave the meetings to attend to them. Meetings of the central management groups are, in this second year, repeatedly rescheduled, signifying shifting priorities. Word has gone round that the RDA is to concentrate on economic regeneration, and this is seen as requiring less interest in

community-based regeneration, however dubious such an assumption would seem to those who really understand the latter. To steal a biblical analogy, the seed of enthusiasm for community participation has in some cases fallen on shallow soil, flourished briefly and is about to wither away unless action is taken fast to improve the soil quality." (Frances Heywood, report, May 2002)

Communities in particular stressed the need for Yorkshire Forward to be stronger in its ruling on the implementation of the benchmarking tool (on the basis that without a stringent assessment process *most* schemes will say that they support community participation). There are complaints that there is 'no bottom line'. Schemes have asked how the RDA will evaluate and use the information it collects from schemes and the extent to which the benchmarking process is contractual and therefore obligatory. Many people living in regeneration communities, alongside schemes that are conscientiously using the benchmarking tool, believe that Yorkshire Forward needs to be more challenging:

> "*Active partners* was a prerequisite of funding for SRB 6 but the RDA does not seem to have the inclination or the teeth to clamp down on those not doing anything."

There have also been questions asked about how Yorkshire Forward is using the benchmarks to measure its own practice and performance and the impact that it has on local regeneration.

> "They need to understand the impact of their role on community participation, for example how long it takes for things to happen and the knock-on effects of things like delays in getting delivery plans signed off."

In the South West, there was a very strong theme in the nine pilot towns event of May 2002, where we were offered examples of projects being signed off but communities being told that they would not get any money for more than nine months.

The need for incentives to implement the benchmarking tool has been raised, particularly at the levels where implementation is not a financial criteria. The idea of 'Beacon Schemes'

for community participation has been suggested – where enhanced funding becomes available as a result of good practice in community participation.

> "If there had been a reward for including gypsies or…. It would be great if a bonus came if they went a step further. Rather than just saying there are a lot of Chinese people but…." (Frances Heywood, Research Team Reflections Day, 22 November 2002)

This points once again to the need to see the tools as not being an end in themselves.

On balance, as far as the partnerships themselves are concerned (and the statutory authorities, quangos and public agencies that are part of them), it is our view that it should be an absolute requirement that there be an audit of community participation. Agencies of this sort are happiest with arrangements that are clearly specified. If it is required, they will let the auditor in. But, compulsion is not enough. Scheme managers work within a world where "everything is compulsory" and they are well used to prioritising all of the compulsory things that they have to do. If there is any ambiguity in the message that is put out by the lead regeneration agency or partnership then the audit will inevitably be de-prioritised, so there has to be an unambiguous political commitment to community participation. Considerable attention will also have to be given to carrots and sticks. If failing to assess community participation is linked to a reduction in income, then people will carry out an assessment. Likewise if there are explicit incentives to assess, this will make it more attractive.

A similar process should apply to community groups who receive funding. We believe that they should be required (a) to give feedback to the initiative in events such as the whole day pilot town events which were held in the South West; and (b) to commit to engaging in a learning network or action inquiry process that supports a process of continuous evaluation. This need not be directly based on the tools, but would almost certainly cover territory that is highlighted by them.

But we must be realistic about the limits to compulsion. Where voluntary effort is concerned, there can never be absolute compulsion. In the South West pilots, the researcher was 'let in' because she had been sent by the RDA, but she did not feel that this was a good footing on which to begin the relationship. She felt that it would have been better if the central management group had asked for volunteer towns to take part in the pilot audit.

All of this would give a strong degree of comparability to assessment of community participation, and would signal the serious intent of government officials and policy makers to make it a core part of programme outcome assessment.

Mainstreaming audit and development processes

It is clear from our pilots that if this work is to have more than a fragmented and marginal impact, it needs to be mainstreamed into the core work of major agencies and departments. One model for this has been described above in the way in which the benchmarking process has been integrated into Yorkshire Forward's work.

Nationally there is a need to roll out a consistent assessment framework across departments and initiatives.

The new assessment framework, *Making community participation meaningful*, has been developed on the back of three years of road testing. Key central government departments and regional agencies have been involved in its development through the steering group. The indicators in the original audit tool have been integrated into the Audit Commission's library of indicators for community participation. This would suggest the possibility that a cross-departmental initiative could be launched by government, which could provide support to the implementation of these tools in different sectors. This might comprise a number of elements:

- A *website* could be constructed which make the tools available on-line, and a team could be made available to provide support.
- A *development programme* could be launched to give a large number of professionals the training and support that they need to carry out the action research facilitation work on the ground.
- Formal audit processes could use the new framework as a *cross-departmental assessment tool*, which could be applied to processes as diverse as best value reviews and evaluations of major neighbourhood renewal programmes.

Conditions

4

In this chapter we outline as succinctly as possible the key findings of the research:

1. The content and focus of both *Active partners* and the *Community participation audit* were largely seen to be comprehensive and useful by stakeholders, partnership boards and community members.

2. The layout of the tools needed to change so that people were able to write into the tables directly and rewrite them to be context specific, ensuring that they were appropriate to particular groups (for example, young people, particular BME groups) or areas (for example, rural as opposed to urban).

3. The language of both of the tools was at times seen to be too jargonistic, and where appropriate the new handbook has been rewritten to take account of this.

4. The most difficult issue to arise from the road testing was how to gain and sustain community and institutional engagement and commitment to the process. Once people were committed, the tools worked, but there was always a great struggle for time. This sort of work does not fit well in small time slots that are part of a longer agenda.

5. Making the audit/benchmarking process compulsory will not *secure* compliance because groups are used to weighing up priorities and deciding which of the many compulsory things that they have to do they will focus on. However, a degree of compulsion is necessary, and if it is linked to sanctions and rewards, the process has a better chance of succeeding. Having a framework that was institutionally supported did enable the researchers in

Yorkshire and the Humber much better access than they might have had if the process was not compulsory. It is our view that institutions and partnerships should be assessed by government with direct reference to a framework of this type. They should have to go through an audit of community participation with as much rigour as they do management, financial and governance audits and should be held accountable for the outcome.

6. Both partnerships and community organisations should be required to show that they are engaged in developmental learning activities and to demonstrate how these have enhanced community participation. It should be noted that communities had a much stronger conceptual grasp of the issues raised by the tools than many professionals. Supporting learning opportunities for professionals around these issues must be seen as of the highest priority.

7. Institutional leadership and commitment was seen to be critical to the success of both the tools. A strong observation in the context of both projects was that the leadership from the lead agency (the RDA in both Yorkshire and the Humber and the South West) gave the appearance of falling away as economic priorities began to take root. This has the effect of making people in localities question whether to make the tools a priority when they do not believe community participation to be a priority of the RDA.

8. It is often not what is recorded in the first instance that is important in the evaluation process. Rather, it is the conversations that it opens up. The level of detail that both tools offer is necessary in order to hold

institutions to account and to be 'meaningful'. But in order to engage with this level of detail, the work needs to be carried out in chunks. This means that it needs to be part of an ongoing developmental process. All of this requires a process that is facilitated. This in turn requires that support be given to the development of skilled community practitioners (either professionals or activists). There may be some merit in exploring how possible it is to set up a facilitators' unit, which could provide support to facilitators carrying out this work.

9. Further, the most effective outcomes are achieved where the tools are not used on their own, but are part of a wider process that involves observation, political advocacy and intervention, interviews, and so on. In other words, they need to sit within a wider action research framework.

10. As a result of this road testing we became aware that large-scale community-based initiatives of the type that we were working with in both regions need a far higher level of core infrastructure support. There is a need for far greater investment in administrative time, dedicated managerial support and sustainable community development resources.

11. The two tools had a slightly different focus, but they were compatible and we have mapped out how they can overlay each other to provide the basis for a more comprehensive combined tool. This will be published as a companion handbook to this research. Our work also needs to connect with other indicators that are being developed elsewhere. One of the clear messages from both community activists and professionals is that there are too many indicators and performance assessment frameworks. We have a great deal of work to do to bring these together, otherwise a combination of confusion and initiative overload will undo our work before we have properly begun.

12. Our work made explicit the problems with separating community and organisational development from benchmarking and assessment. These need to be integrated into the same process, which is why an action research framework for this sort of work is vital.

13. It is worth restating that these tools are not only there to examine the micro-dynamics of particular neighbourhoods; they are important vehicles for constructing local policy, and need to be explicitly linked to the policy development process.

14. If the government is serious about mainstreaming community participation, and accepts our rationale that participation needs to be developed and assessed as rigorously as management and finance, then it needs to take the issue of mainstreaming seriously. We would recommend:
   • investment in development and support for facilitation;
   • a coordinated approach to assessing participation across government departments and the like – based on the framework outlined in the companion handbook to this;
   • a cross-departmental governmental website to make this and other tools available, and to enable practitioner dialogues and problems solving.

Appendix A:
Some broader reflections on what was learned about community participation along the way

The purpose of this piece of work was not to research community participation per se but to assess how well the tools worked and what needed to change. Nevertheless, the intensive and prolonged nature of our work allowed us to gain some insight into the general state of participation policy and practice as it is represented in partnership working today. As with all such work, it represents only a partial snapshot. Nevertheless, there are some issues that need highlighting or restating. The following gives a flavour of what we found.

Professional domination

Regeneration processes still feel very top-down. The employment of staff to support initiatives is nearly always through the local authority or development agency, not by the partnership or other partners. SRB schemes are driven by local authorities, with project funding going in the main to statutory bodies to support top-down initiatives (often the pet schemes of the local authority) rather than community-owned projects. Community activists feel their input and capacity to deliver projects is not recognised. 'Community' is used as a 'right-on' word, but the language used in documents, the complexity of funding regimes, the amount of time to write bids, and so on, excludes community groups. In a competitive bidding situation, the short timescales mean that the process is in danger of becoming worker-led, with the projects of smaller groups being overlooked by larger groups' projects. This can have a particularly devastating effect in relation to BME groups

whose organisational infrastructure is often less developed, and time is a critical factor in supporting and developing participation. The South West MCTI bravely tried to develop a model for participation that was not based on competitive bidding, but this ethos remained embedded in the culture of traditional regeneration and was hard to break both at a professional and community level. Groups have for many years worked within a system where local objectives were partially or wholly adjusted to fit funding streams. Unlearning these habits of behaviour is not easy, and will happen only if the funding agencies hold fast to the new approach.

People in regeneration communities cited the existence of political barriers to their involvement: "too many individuals trying to hang on to power". They also felt that there was no real partnership, with 'last-minute' communication and not enough time given for meaningful consultation.

> "The public and private sectors sometimes think that talking to community reps, networks and forums equals consultation."

A recurring theme was that, too often, representatives from voluntary organisations or umbrella community organisations are taken to be the voice of the community. Tokenism is clearly an issue; "at present SRB working groups seem to be there to rubber stamp lead bodies". Some schemes in Yorkshire still have little or no community representation. Similarly, in parts of the South West, the groups are almost entirely professionally based.

Black and minority ethnic participation

The tools enabled the identification of some important issues with regard to BME participation. There is a strong tendency for partnerships to work with umbrella organisations that can only ever be partially representative. There is a need for partnerships to make direct contact with groups, and to make sure that there is contact with all groups. As one questionnaire return pointed out, "There are two Bangladeshi organisations in Sandwell (with very different views)".

Because of high birth rates among a number of BME groups, the population may be radically skewed towards young people – a group with whom it is particularly hard to gain involvement. In one population group, over 25% were under 16 years of age. This suggests the need for a completely different participation strategy if these groups are to be reached. As the MEL report points out:

"BME groups have a younger age structure than the white population, with young people from minority ethnic backgrounds being disproportionately at risk of experiencing most of the problems of deprivation and social exclusion." (MEL, 2002)

"School exclusion rates for black pupils are significantly higher than for others." (MEL, 2002)

One of the strongest issues to emerge from the questionnaires is that where progress has been made with regard to BME participation, it is often very partial. As one professional respondent pointed out: "It is creditable that the majority of community and residential representatives are from BME communities, ie, 10 out of 12 representatives. Of the 10, nine are from an Afro-Caribbean background". This can leave other communities without a voice. Similarly, a very consistent message from the questionnaires was that women from BME groups are seriously under-represented.

We mentioned in this report the issue of infrastructure. In order for many BME communities to engage effectively with any aspect of community participation, let alone the audit process, they need to increase their capacity (staffing and systems).

There are a number of key issues that the tools must orient themselves towards. While the research pointed out that there are a number of issues that are of specific concern to BME communities, a real danger in practice has been the marginalisation of BME participation to these issues alone. BME participants are often not engaged in the wider regeneration issues.

Resources for participation

Senior partners are often not prepared to devolve enough power and spend enough money to make participation work. One example cited was the difficulty encountered in devolving a community-chest budget to a community panel. Resourcing community participation is a big issue – there is a lack of support for communication between community groups and to pass information across communities. People say they are offered 'shoddy' resources and that there is little recognition that people need expenses payments for travel and childcare if they are to participate and that "even meeting rooms cost money and so does postage, telephone etc".

There is little consideration given within either regeneration programmes or the delivering bodies (funders and partnerships) to the knowledge and skills required to expand community involvement. There are also examples of the responsibility for community participation being passed to administrative workers with no specific skills or understanding of this specialist area of work. Similarly, as we have indicated above, much of this work goes to 'executive officers' who have no background in community development. The infrastructure support to community practice is seriously inadequate to the task.

Equal opportunities policies are usually in place but there are few opportunities for training or support to put the policies into effective practice. There is a lack of information available in community languages and there are not enough

BME workers employed on regeneration schemes.

Clearly, there is a need for real long-term resources – not just benchmarks – if some of the identified barriers (organisational culture and structures, financial restrictions, unrealistic funding deadlines and procedures, power held centrally/controlled by local politicians, balancing strategic work with day-to-day running) to implementation are to be overcome.

'Community' organisation

Meetings are often not inclusive – sometimes because of a lack of community confidence and sometimes because of deliberate exclusion. We saw examples of meetings being called at short notice with no consultation about what was already happening locally and meetings being held in inaccessible venues. Some community representatives found that the minutes of meetings did not always adequately reflect issues raised by them. Equally, not everyone wanted to attend meetings.

"Anyone who does not attend or even see the advert for the meeting may have no opportunity to be informed."

There is a lack of clarity about who community representatives 'represent' and they are rarely given the support, resources and mechanisms to help them to feed back to their constituency. Community representation is sometimes dominated by those who are middle class, 'articulate' and not intimidated by the surroundings where meetings are held. The community is sometimes represented by 'hand-picked puppets' and voluntary sector gatekeepers. One person has commented that "community bullies are rife and increasing".

Information and communication

Information is lacking or is not in a suitable format for all members of the community. People feel that they only receive selective information. This lack of information leads to lack of power to influence. Jargon is a barrier to people's ability to participate. Networking can often benefit those who already have the most power – it is not what you know but who you know. In the South West, information and communication were consistently highlighted as the greatest area of weakness in the initiatives – in particular, communication between the central management and the officers who are supposed to implement the programme but who are not adequately briefed, and the community groups themselves. In a way, this is surprising because, at face value, it should be one of the easier things to get right.

Appendix B:
Ideas for practice from the Yorkshire and the Humber pilot

Ideas for practice related to the benchmarking tools have included the following:

Benchmarks	Ideas for practice
The community is recognised and valued as an equal partner at all stages of the process	• Involve local people when identifying and interviewing contractors/staff. • Beware of 'He/she who shouts loudest wins!' – it is important that partnerships are developed where every voice is heard. • Rights and obligations should be built into terms of reference to provide for equality of partnership.
There is meaningful community representation on all decision-making bodies	• Aim for a certain percentage level of representation – appropriate to context/starting point. • Keep meetings as informal as possible. • Create umbrella groups, thus representing smaller groups, but also having a bigger voice and more influence. • Elect representatives through public meetings and postal ballots.
All community members have the opportunity to participate	• Consider different points of contact, eg surgeries/clinics. • Develop an employers'/business forum. • Develop specific projects and provide skills to engage all communities. • Set up themed community networks. • Enable children and young people to take responsibility for their future.
Communities have access to and control over resources	• Project workers include those with community development skills. • Regeneration teams must be locally based. It helps if some team members are locally recruited. • Work on changing attitudes.
Evaluation of regeneration partnerships incorporates a community agenda	• Ensure employment of local people in research and evaluation processes, eg 'On our Doorstep' – Royds, Bradford. • Evaluation should be ongoing. 'Routeways to Success' has an approach of alerting workers to the impact of their work. • Ensure questions are asked from a community perspective.
The diversity of local communities and interests are reflected at all levels of the regeneration process	• Carry out a baseline study of involvement, ie active/dormant communities. • Have an agreed legal framework to ensure accountability. • Use co-options to ensure a diversity of community involvement. • Use sub-groups and invite local people to take part.

Benchmarks	Ideas for practice
Equal opportunities policies are in place and implemented	• Apply to staff, community members and board members. • Rebadge equal opportunities to ensure discussion of anti-discriminatory practices. • Provide training programmes.
Unpaid workers/volunteer activists are valued	• Make annual awards, eg 'community activist of the year'. • Provision of training – establish a 'learning fund' to fund training. • Implement a policy of employing local people – provide advice, support and encouragement to unpaid activists to seek paid jobs within the scheme. • Provide induction packs for paid staff and volunteers.
A two-way information strategy is developed and implemented	• Where there are a variety of partnerships within a locality, use one publication to avoid duplication and bombardment. • Have community representatives on editorial boards of newsletters. • Produce an annual regeneration report for residents in the format of a calendar, using photos taken by young people. • Produce community newsletters regularly, in local community languages. • Produce community information packs for organisations. • Establish a residents' resource library. • Evaluate all publicity material – link to 'Communicate with Confidence' course for residents. • Hold regular topic group meetings rotated around the area.
Programme and project procedures are clear and in accessible	• Make board and other meetings open to the public. • Provide plain language 'guidance notes' for appraisal and monitoring forms. • Provide one-to-one sessions on form filling. • Involve community groups in designing application forms.
Communities are resourced to participate	• 'Futures Fund' (URBAN, Sheffield) supports networking and attendance at conferences throughout Britain. • A capacity-building project for young people has been extremely creative in involving them in decision making (Leeds Initiative). • Employ and train local people to reach out to excluded groups. • Provide support for people to write bids and business plans. • Provide guidance and assistance with fundraising. • Provide administrative support for community activists.
Understanding, knowledge and skills are developed to support partnership working	• Translate statements into action (at the pace of people's knowledge and understanding). • Carry out training needs analysis. • Encourage partners to market themselves to one another.

C

Appendix C:
Project reports

Because of the nature of this project, many reports were generated along the way summarising activities and outcomes both for ourselves and for various steering groups who we were working with. The following are some of the key ones:

Burns, D. and Taylor, M. (2000) Auditing community participation: An assessment handbook, Bristol/York: The Policy Press/ Joseph Rowntree Foundation.

COGS (2002) *Assessing community involvement in regeneration: Report for Danny Burns*, May.

Ferron-Smith, C. (2002) *Report on BME community participation: Analysis report*, July.

Heywood, F. (2002) *Bottom up meets top down: Final report to the Regional Management Group of the South West Market and Coastal Towns Initiative on the audit of community participation*, June.

Heywood, F. (2002) *The Market and Coastal Towns project in Minehead: A view from the audit of community participation*, February.

MEL (2002) *Increasing black and ethnic minority community participation in regeneration*.

Wilson, M. and Wilde, P. (2003) *Benchmarking community participation: Developing and implementing the Active partners benchmarks*, York: Joseph Rowntree Foundation.

Appendix D:
Key contacts

This report has highlighted the importance of developing auditing and benchmarking community participation work within an action research/action learning framework. Readers who are interested in pursuing this aspect of the work in more detail can contact **SOLAR**, at the University of the West of England, Bristol, UK. SOLAR, which stands for Social and Organisational Learning as Action Research, is a research and development team specialising in large system action research. It is codirected by Danny Burns. For more information contact solar@uwe.ac.uk or visit their website on www.uwe.ac.uk/solar

COGS Consultancy (Communities and Organisations: Growth and Support) specialises in participatory development of planning and analysis frameworks and tools. Contact COGS Directors Mandy Wilson and Pete Wilde via mail@cogs.solis.co.uk

The **Active Partners Unit** was established in the final stage of the *Active partners* road-testing work by COGS and is located within the regional forum for Yorkshire and the Humber, info@activepartners.org.uk

Also available from The Policy Press
Published in association with the Joseph Rowntree Foundation

Making community participation meaningful:
A handbook for development and assessment
Danny Burns, Frances Heywood, Marilyn Taylor, Pete Wilde and Mandy Wilson

This handbook is a companion volume to *What works in assessing community participation?* (The Policy Press, 2004) which documents the results of the road testing of two earlier frameworks for assessing community participation – *Active partners: Benchmarking community participation in regeneration* (Yorkshire Forward, 2000) and *Auditing community participation: An assessment handbook* (The Policy Press, 2000).

Making community participation meaningful:
- outlines key considerations that are necessary to ensure that community participation is effective;
- provides detailed sets of questions to enable stakeholders to assess the extent to which the indicators of success are being met;
- highlights a variety of resources which can be used by community groups to generate information and insight into the key issues.

A4 Report • £14.95 (US$25.50) • ISBN 1 86134 614 X • 76 pages • July 2004

To order further copies of this publication or any other Policy Press titles please contact:

In the UK and Europe:
Marston Book Services, PO Box 269 Abingdon,
Oxon, OX14 4YN, UK
Tel: +44 (0)1235 465500
Fax: +44 (0)1235 465556,
Email: direct.orders@marston.co.uk

In the USA and Canada:
ISBS, 920 NE 58th Avenue, Suite 300,
Portland, OR 97213-3786, USA
Tel: +1 800 944 6190 (toll free)
Fax: +1 503 280 8832,
Email: info@isbs.com

In Australia and New Zealand:
DA Information Services, 648 Whitehorse Road
Mitcham, Victoria 3132, Australia
Tel: +61 (3) 9210 7777
Fax: +61 (3) 9210 7788,
E-mail: service@dadirect.com.au

Further information about all of our titles can be found on our website

www.policypress.org.uk

Author contact details

SOLAR, at the University of the West of England, Bristol, UK. SOLAR, which stands for Social and Organisational Learning as Action Research, is a research and development team specialising in large system action research. It is codirected by Danny Burns. For more information contact solar@uwe.ac.uk or visit their website on www.uwe.ac.uk/solar

COGS Consultancy (Communities and Organisations: Growth and Support) specialises in participatory development of planning and analysis frameworks and tools. Contact COGS Directors Mandy Wilson and Pete Wilde via mail@cogs.solis.co.uk